Power
and the
Police Chief

STUDIES IN CRIME, LAW, AND JUSTICE

Series Editor: James A. Inciardi,
Division of Criminal Justice, University of Delaware

Studies in Crime, Law, and Justice contains original research formulations and new analytic perspectives on continuing important issues of crime and the criminal justice and legal systems. Volumes are research based but are written in nontechnical language to allow for use in courses in criminal justice, criminology, law, social problems, and related subjects.

Power
and the
Police Chief

An Institutional and Organizational Analysis

Raymond G. Hunt
John M. Magenau

SCLJ · 10
Studies in Crime, Law, and Justice

SAGE Publications
International Educational and Professional Publisher
Newbury Park   London   New Delhi

For information address:

SAGE Publications, Inc.
2455 Teller Road
Newbury Park, California 91320

SAGE Publications Ltd.
6 Bonhill Street
London EC2A 4PU
United Kingdom

SAGE Publications India Pvt. Ltd.
M-32 Market
Greater Kailash I
New Delhi 110 048 India

Printed in the United States of America

Library of Congress Cataloging-in-Publication Data

Hunt, Raymond G., 1928-
  Power and the police chief: an institutional and organizational
analysis / by Raymond G. Hunt, John M. Magenau.
      p.   cm.   —(Studies in crime, law, and justice ; v. 10)
  Includes bibliographical references (p.   ) and index.
  ISBN 0-8039-4654-6 (cl).   —ISBN 0-8039-4655-4 (pb)
  1. Police chiefs—United States. 2. Police—United States.
I. Magenau, John M. II. Title. III. Series.
HV8141.H85 1993
350.74'068'4—dc20   92-43389

93 94 95 96 10 9 8 7 6 5 4 3 2 1

Sage Production Editor: Tara S. Mead

Contents

Preface

The police and their agencies are important and powerful fixtures of societies. What the police do and how they do it is worth the attention of scholars and every other citizen, for it bears heavily on the character and quality of people's lives. Police chiefs, in particular, are at once the specific instruments who shape and direct the actions of the local police departments that impinge immediately upon a citizenry; and, more generally, they are molders of their societies.

Great as their power may be, however, the police and their chiefs are constrained in society by parties and conditions not easily subject to their comprehension much less their command.

In a September 9, 1992, article in *The New York Times,* under the headline "Washington Chief Joins a Trend of Frustration," Felicity Barringer reported the retirement of Isaac Fulwood, Jr., after 3 years at the head of the police force in the country's "most heavily policed and murder-prone city" (p. B8). The *Times* went on to observe that "big-city chiefs are pulling out of intractable wars . . . tired and beat up from the strain." Noting that New York, Los Angeles, San Francisco, San Jose, Houston, Philadelphia, Detroit, and Austin all had lost chiefs in the year past (not all of them departing voluntarily), the *Times* suggested that murder rates, drug wars, falling budgets, and political turnover were leaving chiefs "struggling against the tide."

This book is about the nature, causes, and consequences of this struggle. It is not, however, about murder rates, drug wars, or falling budgets. Instead it deals with the complex and less tangible social and political forces that shape the police, their agencies, and the local environments in which they operate.

In one of the better books on policing by an "insider," Anthony ("Tony") Bouza, the recently retired Minneapolis Police Chief, challenged the police "to open the agency and develop a common sense of purpose with the public they are hired to protect and serve." Bouza also challenged that public "to understand the institution of the police in order to make sensible decisions about it" (1990, p. 84).

Our aim for this book is to help meet Bouza's challenges by advancing an appreciation of the developing institutions of American policing and of the changing organizational circumstances in which the police and others work and interact with an interested citizenry in a democratic community. Like Bouza, who has advised police executives that they need to understand their societies if they are "to function effectively in a highly political role" (p. 238), we are led by our analyses to reflect upon the evolving role of the now and future police chief as, wittingly or not, an inevitable instrument of change in police culture.

We cast the police and their leaders as local actors in wider social settings that steadily change. Long-term rationalist modernization of the Western world has not exempted American police agencies. Rather, as we describe in the first part of the book, it has politicized and transformed them and the police chief's role. Simultaneous tendencies toward the professionalization and bureaucratization of police work have polarized relations between police chiefs and rank and file officers and have precipitated internal and external conflicts and local power wars that, we suggest, have converted police organizations into contemporary political arenas.

We use this political arena metaphor in the second part of the book, along with theoretical discussion and case examples, to explore the power position of the contemporary police chief in relation to other players in the American police network. Special attention is given to conflicts among chiefs, police rank and file, and their associations as primary antagonists in an institutional contest for control of the normative bases of police work and police organizations. We find the roots of this contest in long-term societal forces working toward the rational transformation of police work and of the local agencies suitable to its organization and regulation.

At stake in the political arenas of contemporary American policing, then, is the fundamental definition of *police work.* Modernization has begot new paradigms of policing that now would move it away from the rule-based law-enforcement models predominant during the first half of the American 20th Century toward service and order maintenance alternatives that emphasize the situational imperatives and discretionary essence of police work "on the street." In perhaps surprising commonality with the "total quality management" movements now widespread in the business world, these trends imply basic changes in the culture of policing; and, for police chiefs, they bring new roles and challenges that have more to do with visionary leadership than with traditional administration, roles that demand from them new attitudes and skills.

At one or another time and in one or another way, many people have contributed to our efforts to understand the police, police work, and police chiefs. Some of them have saved us from error (or maybe tried and failed) by reading and commenting on our writing; others have helped us gather and interpret information; and others have simply been encouraging (or patient). For these things, we are grateful to John Delaney, Virginia Fails, Peter Feuille, Lee Griffin, Hubert Locke, Peter Manning, Gary Marx, Karen McCadden, Jim Meindl, Simon Singer, Judy Shippengrover, Jim Sterling, and Mary Ann Wycoff. Most especially, we owe thanks for their help, tolerance, and instruction to the many police officers, police chiefs, and federal, state, and local officials with whom we have worked throughout the country during the past 15 years or so.

Some of the research from which this book benefitted was supported by grants from the National Science Foundation, the National Institute for Mental Health, and the National Institute of Justice, as well as by our employers, the State University of New York at Buffalo and Penn State Erie, The Behrend College.

Raymond G. Hunt
Buffalo, New York

John M. Magenau
Erie, Pennsylvania

PART I

Institutional Change in Policing

1

Introduction

Not much is known about police chiefs, which illustrates what the former Commissioner of Police in Syracuse, Detroit, Washington, and New York (and later President of the Police Foundation), Patrick Murphy (1977), called the "Lone Ranger" quality of American policing. In a search of the literature since 1900, Lewis Mayo (1985), a training director at the National Institute of Justice, found a smattering of autobiographies but otherwise uncovered only five book-length studies of police chiefs, one of them (the most recent) his own 1983 doctoral dissertation. The pace of publishing in this area may have quickened a bit since 1985, but still, when compared with the volume of research on line officers, the research literature on chiefs remains minuscule (Mayo, 1985, p. 398).

Even writings by chiefs and former chiefs often are only indirectly informative about their roles. For instance, in his book on police administration, Anthony ("Tony") Bouza (1978), the now-retired police commissioner of Minneapolis, emphasized the political and administrative functions of police executives and argued that the police chief executive officer (CEO) should be a civilian "serving at the pleasure of the executive of the city" (p. 232), but he otherwise said surprisingly little about exactly what a police chief does. This is typical. Even Wycoff's (1982) exemplary study of the role of municipal police, which largely summed up knowledge on the subject, had virtually nothing to say specifically about chiefs. Wycoff's focus on rank-and-file activity provides a fundamental framework of operational knowledge for thinking about administrative roles but gives no information about how those roles are actually structured or implemented.

Modern works on police administration, beginning with August Vollmer (1936/1971) and O. W. Wilson (1963), have generally been more prescriptive than descriptive. They focus on delineating *functions* that somehow must be served in police organizations—patrol, investigations, inspections, personnel, supervision, and so on—and suggest that police chiefs are responsible for ensuring that they are done well, adding perhaps some information about modern management methods. None of this gives an especially vivid picture of the particular empirical qualities of a police chief's role.

In his magnum opus *Commissioner*, Murphy (1977) does give a vivid picture of one chief at work: himself. As helpful as it and other similar memoirs are in giving a feel for the occupation of police executive, Murphy's story, naturally, is the story of Pat Murphy and the sometimes dramatic or picaresque episodes that helped shape his views on policing; views he unambiguously discloses in the book. Anecdotal testimonies such as *Commissioner* and Daryl Gates's (1992) reminiscence on his life in the Los Angeles Police Department (LAPD) are fascinating, of course, for what they reveal about the people and places involved, giving us a peek behind the mask of one or another Lone Ranger. Bouza's (1990) more recent book, *The Police Mystique,* does the same thing (and, as we show later, quite a bit more). Collectively, such works as these can provide the reader with some genuine insights into the nature of the practices and practitioners of police work.

Our book is a study of these practices, their practitioners, and their associated relationships—a study, in short, of the American police chief's role, primarily in its institutional aspects. More precisely, the book is an institutional treatment of American police that focuses on its leadership—that is, on the person and function of the police chief.

Broadly speaking, this involves our viewing the police, police agencies, and police leadership in their societal contexts, while giving special attention to the processes and effects of modernization in American police agencies. From this institutional perspective (which we soon describe more fully), we depict an associated managerial transformation of the police chief's role, together with tendencies toward the professionalization and bureaucratization of police work. In doing so, we highlight the internal and external conflicts and power struggles that have converted contemporary police departments into a sort of organizational species that Henry Mintzberg (1983) aptly calls "political arenas." Then, in the second part of the book, we explore manifestations of these societal power struggles in police organizations.

In this book, we use the title *police chief* generically to mean simply a head of a locally organized police agency. This individual may bear any of a number of titles in the United States: *Chief, commissioner,* and *sheriff* are the most common. The organizations headed by these chiefs vary greatly in size and complexity, from two or three persons to thousands. Obviously, not all of them are alike. Indeed, that they are not alike is a premise of this book. Local police departments reflect their particular local contexts. Therefore, though it is not actually necessary, it is probably wise to limit the reach of the analyses that follow to chiefs in larger, more formally structured organizations, where the action of institutional forces is apt to be clearer. In subsequent chapters, we review the changing nature of police work and organization, and the contentious quality of the change. From a local craft-based and semifeudal traditional organization, the argument runs, cosmo-politan institutional forces have worked toward a bureaucratic modern-ization of police roles and police organizations around rational norms. These transformational pressures have induced strongly politicized reactions and internal-external contests for control of police functions and struc-tures. The result is a contemporary political arena in which police chiefs are the central figures beset on all sides by contending interests, working sometimes to transform the nature and forms of policing, and at other times to conserve existing patterns and traditions.

This is not a case study, but, in order to illuminate its arguments and provide grounding for its analyses, case excerpts are scattered throughout the text. These excerpts have been drawn not exclusively but mostly from observations made during a 3-year study of decision making by police in six U.S. cities (see Hunt & Magenau, 1983a), and a separate multiyear action-research effort on institutional racism in law enforcement, involving a different set of six U.S. cities (see Hunt, 1987).[1] Naturally, we have attached fictitious names to the places and persons described in these cases.

NOTE

1. These projects were supported, respectively, by NSF Grant No. 05577-24548, and NIMH Grant No. 1 R01 MH30522-01.

2

The Institutional Perspective

When we refer to an "institutional perspective" on the police chief, we mean that we wish to understand police and police leadership in terms of their accommodations to the social contexts or environments in which they are embedded. Together with their histories, these contexts shape the particular features of individual agencies and their leadership, including even the mundane aspects of their operations.

In an eastern U.S. city, for example, a seemingly routine and altogether internal decision on adopting a new nightstick nevertheless actively took into account the following: (a) its cost (which was not great); (b) its legal implications (which seemed favorable because fewer injuries were expected); (c) local political considerations (which seemed negligible because the new equipment was not much different from the old); and (d) the item's symbolic value (which was quite important, for the weapon was arguably defensive rather than offensive, and there had been allegations of unnecessary police force involving batons); independent of these allegations, a citizen's committee had recommended training officers in alternatives to deadly force, and the department wished to appear responsive to all of these alternatives.

This routine example shows this eastern city's attentiveness to ordinary practicalities (e.g., costs) in its decision making and also its sensitivity to its social and political context. Concerns with legalities, politics, symbolism, and community constituencies all are external institutional concerns that complicate even seemingly simple organizational decisions. They reflect pressures generated outside a particular police agency, by the law or by other sources of widespread authority (Zucker, 1987, p. 447)—that is, by institutions.

THE NATURE OF INSTITUTIONS

By definition, institutional analyses concentrate attention on societal institutions. Precisely what this means, however, remains unsettled. Scott

(1987), for one, has pointed out that the vital concepts *institution* and *institutionalization* both lack standard definitions. Consequently, there is variation in what institutional analysts analyze and how. Nevertheless, it is plain enough that institutional theory is an external perspective on organizations. As Parsons (1960) insisted, organizations—police departments included —are never to be regarded entirely apart from their environments.

Still, Kingsley Davis (1950) long ago made plain that *institutions* are abstractions, "not tangible things like stones" (p. 515). Defining them as "sets of interwoven folkways, mores and laws built around one or more functions" (p. 71), Davis emphasized the ambiguity of the concept, pointing to the loose coupling of institutional elements plus the fact that verbal formulations of normative systems typically are superficial. Nevertheless, he argued that the concept of *institution* serves better than any other to convey the order and interdependent segmentation of a society's normative structures. Albeit no modern society can be expected to exhibit either consistency or constancy in its normative order, an *institutional system* is one that more or less clearly specifies the rules of legitimation it uses and the ways in which those rules are expressed in social interactions.

Legitimacy simply means "rightful" or "justified." Implied, of course, is some sustaining standard: customs, laws, processes (e.g., reason or logic). Institutions, in other words, become institutions by passing a test of legitimacy, the normative standards of which the institutions both meet and express. In the modern era, these standards (as we show in Chapter 3) have become primarily matters of rationality, largely in a functional or pragmatic form, at least in America.

HOW INSTITUTIONS BECOME INSTITUTIONS

Smelser (1988) described the process of institutionalization as a social construction of reality, a kind of externalization of routines, which thereupon are perceived and passed on to others as objective realities. Presumably, this process is rooted in people's needs to make sense of their worlds and to fit the different pieces of it into larger, internally consistent normative theories that explain events while guiding action. Practices are institutionalized when they acquire a status beyond that of personal preference and become customary within a community: simple things such as saying "thank you" for a gift, more elaborate things such as the game of baseball or the process of electing the President of the United States, and attitudinal things such as deference to a police officer.

Within an institutionalist framework, particular organizations may be variously understood as *artifacts* (i.e., as expressions of the things and ideas—the shared realities—that are taken for granted within a society [Selznick, 1957]) or, perhaps less instrumentally, as further features of a socially constructed reality (i.e., as abstractions that take on objective qualities by a process of externalizing collective norms—symbols, customs, and beliefs—and perhaps imbuing them with a moral quality as well [Van de Ven and Astley, 1981]). In either case, it will be true that institutional analysis is less theoretical than it is postural. It is mainly an attitude or way of viewing organizational and administrative systems in social context—an external perspective on these systems, as we have said—rather than a systematic body of propositions about them.

INSTITUTIONAL THEORY

Perrow (1979) aptly limns the institutionalist posture as (a) an orientation to holistic analysis that seeks to represent the ostensible organic character of social systems; (b) a tendency to stress the uniqueness of organizations and so to be disposed toward case studies and natural histories; and (c) a view of organizations in mutually influential relations with environments. Institutionalists, therefore, typically try to understand organizational activities and outcomes as adaptations to the social contexts in which they are embedded. In contrast, Zucker (1987) has pointed out that institutional theory "is inherently difficult to explicate, because it taps taken-for-granted assumptions at the core of social actions" (p. 443).

Both as phenomena and as sources of influence, institutions have a quasi-objective, social, factlike quality. Vague as this sounds, it simply means that institutions are things experienced as "out there," aspects of an external social reality. Their properties are manifest in more or less standardized formal *structures*—patterns of social action that have a normative quality, in that they are widely distributed in a social network (e.g., a nation) and are generally seen as "right," such as the game of baseball mentioned earlier or offering thanks for a gift.

Obviously, the idea of an institutional order refers to a very general and insistent arrangement of society that defines and controls broad features of social organization, thereby imposing fundamental constraints on local discretion. The specifically normative quality of institutions is shown, say, in the ways in which organizations copy one another, and the actions of formal norm-setting agents, such as the state, the professions, and how-to-do-it textbooks that disseminate the authoritative word about what structures, methods, and modes of conduct are right, proper, good, or in favor, currently—for instance, Total Quality Management (TQM), about which we speak further in Part II of this book.

Institutional influences on local organizations, thus, work to constrain patterns of action separately from immediate technical considerations. "Infused with value," as Selznick (1957) put it, the institutions of society ensure that organizational forms and behaviors will not be entirely a local option, or even a simple function of the task at hand. Modern institutions are, in general, deeply rationalized and organized. Their operating elements —local police departments, for instance—can be expected to follow suit, as we describe in the following chapter.

"Institutional fields," Zucker (1987) has said, "limit the direction and content of change, causing an inexorable push toward homogenization" (p. 452). At the same time, however, organizations and their agents are not necessarily mere passive pawns of their environments, institutional or other. Some of them—at least big and powerful ones—influence both their own environments and the environments of other organizations by affecting societal networks and processes of institutionalization (Scott, 1987).

INSTITUTIONAL POWER AND AUTHORITY

This last feature of institutions—their reciprocating environmental relations—gives point to concerns with power and authority, and to Perrow's complaint about scholars too often occupying themselves with what he considers the trivial organizations of society: for example, mental hospitals that affect only a tiny segment of society, as compared, say, with big businesses or the military-industrial complex (Perrow's examples), which affect everybody. Perrow's point is well taken. It is not just that big businesses directly affect a lot of people that makes them important. What makes them important is that they are powerful vis-à-vis their environments and, therefore, have a better than average potential for influencing those environments and with them the environments of other organizations (and individual people); that is precisely what makes the police, and specifically their leadership, important, and thus partly (at least) explains the interest in them here. Governments, after all, are monopolists of force: the ultimate legitimizers of conduct and enforcers of norms. The police embody and actualize this regulative power, holding as they do, a special charter for its forceful exercise, which we discuss at length later on.

INSTITUTIONAL POLITICS AND
THE PURPOSE OF THIS STUDY

The rest of Perrow's characterizations of institutional analysis (i.e., his first two points, regarding holistic analysis and a focus on organizational uniqueness) may be taken generally to summarize the analytic strategy of this book. In it, we direct attention to the police as a social institution and to the police chief as an institutional actor. We intend to describe the cross-currents, on the one hand, of institutional forces working toward the secular rationalization—the modernization—of police work, and, on the other hand, the immediate demands of tradition-based and technologically based forms of police organization and operation. Our focus, then, is on what may be termed the *institutional politics of policing,* as distinct from (although certainly mixed up with) the more particular interplay of local interests and their advocates. We perceive the police chief, in societal context, to be at once a tangible focal point of institutional change and a kind of lightning rod for its ramified and incendiary local organizational consequences, consequences to which we pay particular attention in the second part of the book.

3

The Meaning of Modernity

We have characterized the institutional changes with which today's police chiefs are entangled by using the word *modernization.* We need now to spell out the meaning of this concept and its expressions in contemporary society, the police included.

Modernity, modernization, and the *modern* are large and imprecise ideas. Their point is to suggest broad epochal contrasts in the ways people and their societies live, think, and act. So just what constitutes *modernity* is a matter of time, place, and perspective. Our modern era, for example, has been characterized as a search for impersonality, for ways of ordering human relations that will separate individual motives from institutional goals while leveling social differences. The nub of the matter in any such characterization is the basic values according to which social arrangements and actions are justified or legitimized among a people. By implication, those values that are modern, and the social structures associated with them, must somehow differ systematically from premodern counterparts.

THE MODERN AND THE PREMODERN

The contemporary differences between modern and premodern eras usually are described in terms of the modern era's more detached reliance on reason, analysis, and the discovery of factual bases for human action. In short, the hallmark of our modern era is the ostensible rationality of its decisions. To rationalize is the essence of modernity.

The achievement of rationality requires a "purging of particularism" from social relations, as Perrow (1979) has put it. *Particularism,* Andrew Walder (1986) suggests, stands at one end (a premodern end) of a spectrum of human relationships, at which a personal element predominates in social relations, and the primary motivation for a specific relationship is the "affective aspect of the tie." Particularism, in practice, "involves showing favoritism toward people with whom one has a preexisting relationship"

(Walder, 1986, p. 179). At the other end, the modern end, of the relational spectrum is what Walder characterizes as a "relationship that amounts to ceremonialized bribery" (p. 180): an impersonal, "universalistic" one in which people exchange favors for money (or any material gain), the motivation for which is instrumental rather than emotional; "contributions" are made in return for "inducements," as Chester Barnard (1938) put it, in an organizational context.

Modernism and Bureaucracy

The modern world, then, is one that idealizes reason, universal norms, emotional neutrality, instrumental values, and specificity of social relationships or roles. All of these ideas resonate in Max Weber's classical characterization of the prototypical "rational-legal" bureaucracy. Nominally ways of sensibly ordering social action, rational-legal bureaucracies rely on a universalistic contractual basis for association rather than on particularistic ones based on emotional ties either to certain persons or to a specific group's traditions.

The hallmark of modern rational-legal bureaucracy is reliance on formal legal bases of authority and due process—deliberation, democracy, analysis—in deciding the conventions of social action. Actors are functionaries or role players carrying out duties defined by positions to which they are allocated but that they do not own. Their rights and responsibilities—their powers—belong to their positions, not to themselves; and the forms of their interactions with others depend on the specified relations of their respective statuses—their ascribed roles—not on their individual characteristics. Obedience in rational-legal bureaucracy is to a rule, not to a person; and positional tenure is subject only to explicit standards of specialized competence. The defining properties of rational-legal bureaucracy are summarized in Table 3.1.

Premodern Bureaucracy

Weber contrasted the universalistic rule-based (modern) norms of rational-legal bureaucracy with two other more particularistic (premodern) varieties: charismatic and traditional. *Charismatic norms* are peculiar to a person: Their normative power—their ability to compel obedience—rests on a follower's devotion and particular attachment to a specific exceptional (e.g., sacred or heroic) leader. *Traditional norms,* on the other hand, are familial or feudal: They are peculiar to a social group and depend on that group's sense of its defining nature and a belief in the sanctity of its history and customs. Traditional leaders are exemplars of these traditions but otherwise are not necessarily special persons.

Table 3.1 Characteristics of Rational-Legal Bureaucracy

Decision making and operation according to rationally derived rules or laws

Formalism—decisions and rules, formulated in writing

Hierarchic organization of specialized offices or roles, based on impersonal rules; supervision of lower offices by higher ones

Technical (rational) rules regulating conduct of offices

Separation of position and authority from the person; no appropriation of position by the person, who has an obligation to perform the duties of the current position

Offices filled on a freely contractual basis

Regulation of fixed duties by laws or rules

Selection, incumbency based on competence: expertise/credentials, standardized systems for assessing competence—tests/diplomas/credentials

Office holding as a vocation/career

Rationalization of preparation—education and training

Pay by money/fixed salaries

NOTE: Based on Henderson and Parsons (1947) and on Gerth and Mills (1946).

Thus legality, charisma, and tradition are alternative means of legitimizing or justifying authority, and the distribution of authority in administrative apparatuses (such as bureaucracies) is a means of codifying power and expressing domination. Hence, alongside modern rational-legal bureaucracies can be arrayed premodern charismatic and traditional bureaucratic forms, and all three of these forms may (and surely do) coexist. It is variation in the *relative* density of different organizational forms (rational-legal, traditional, and charismatic bureaucracies) that defines historical epochs. A modern era (such as ours) is perhaps one where, in general, rational-legal bureaucracy is more common or dominant or respected than are charismatic or traditional forms, but not one, as we show later, where the latter two are unknown or even unvalued.

Weber, in any case, dealt in *ideal types*: expository frameworks or models that were not necessarily expected to be found exactly replicated in reality. There is, in fact, no Weberian argument against finding not only coexisting empirical examples of each of his three bureaucratic forms, but also in- dividual organizations that manifest mixtures of traditional, charismatic, and rational-legal characteristics—and various hybrid forms as well. Indeed, as we have said, such is the reality. (In a later chapter, we speak about one such hybrid, Walder's neo-traditional form.)

Still, as solutions to problems of social control in an increasingly complex world that has grown beyond the effective command of charismatic leaders or the reach of established tradition, rational-legal bureaucracies *and,* more fundamentally, the cultural predominance of their rule-based premises, joined with a contemporary scientific model of reason, make the modern era modern. As true as this proposition is in the abstract, however, the fact is that the temporal boundaries of modern and premodern are not sharply delimited. Modernization does not suddenly or conspicuously appear. Rather like Darwinian evolution, it is a progressive emergent that spans considerable periods of time.

Lawrence Stone (1991), in a review of Paul Johnson's book, *The Birth of the Modern: World Society 1815-30,* wrote as follows on the point (p. 39):

> The world we live in today emerged [not in the 15 years suggested by Johnson, but] in fits and starts stretching over a 300-year period. If we were seriously to seek the origin of the modern world, we would begin with its intellectual foundations laid down by the Renaissance, the Reformation, and the Enlightenment, from which emerged a few dominant ideas, such as a belief in scientific and technological progress, individualism, rationalism, secularism, and religious pluralism. Its technological base was laid in the fifteenth century by the invention of the printing press, which slowly revolutionized the communication of ideas; of gunpowder, which for the first time made it possible to kill people in very large numbers; and of the magnetic compass, which at last made it possible to navigate across the vast oceans of the world. All of these were discovered before the end of the fifteenth century. Nor can the period of 1815-30 be said to have laid the basis for a surplus of food that saved the growing population of Europe from a major Malthusian crisis: the Great Plains of the United States, after all, had not yet been brought under the plow, and the flood of wheat from Chicago across the Atlantic began only in the 1870s.

Weber, too, had found modern analogues in premodern England, Germany, Roman law, and ancient Egypt. What he saw in late-nineteenth century Europe was not, then, a sudden emergence but instead a burgeoning of rationalist social organization in the particular shape of the meritocratic rational-legal bureaucracy and its instrumental emphasis on efficient impersonality. What Weber foresaw, moreover, was its inevitably progressive hegemony, a vision captured by his famous "iron cage" metaphor (as cited in Scaff, 1989, pp. 90-91):

> For the modern individual, action and existence are regimented necessities of vocational activity, now stripped of its sustaining structures of meaning. We are all, as it were, conscripted as unconsenting participants in a universalized vocational culture, our horizons limited to the rationalized, endless, and inwardly meaningless certainties of "vocational humanity." . . . In Weber's view no one can be exempted: "Everywhere the cage for the new serfdom is ready"

and every "developmental tendency" points to its perfection and perma-
nence. . . . Modernity is characterized not just by a kind of petrifaction and
homogenization of external conditions of life, but in addition by inescapable
conflict among the very contents of different value-spheres, life-orders, and
life-powers.

FREDERICK TAYLOR AND THE
MODERN SCIENCE OF MANAGEMENT

Weber's orientation was mainly to the large institutions of society, where
his concern was with their means of legitimizing authority. His view of
the organizations within society was essentially as local power structures
expressive of larger cosmopolitan institutional forces. Weber's American
contemporary, Frederick W. Taylor (1947), on the other hand, concentrated
his attention much more narrowly on the workplace and on organizations
as technical systems where legitimacy questions were decided on the explicit
basis of rational science. Chiefly concerned with eliminating waste in the
expanding industrial enterprises of turn-of-the-century America, Taylor's
principal criterion of rationality was frankly economic. No social philoso-
pher, his aspiration was to devise methods for enhancing the efficiency
of work processes by applying orderly, quantitative scientific methods to
their analysis—hence the label and slogan of his enterprise: "Scientific
Management."

Neither Taylor nor Weber knew the other man's work, but each captured
or expressed facets of the same rational, universalistic themes of modernity. One of them (Weber) was a grand theorist, who saw those themes at
a macroscopic or societal level; the other (Taylor), a practical man, saw
them in the more microscopic setting of the shop floor.

Taylor urged the improvement of enterprise by concentrating on specific
work methods or *processes*. By measuring and analyzing "man-machine"
relations (e.g., via time and methods study), he sought to optimize performance by discovering and then prescribing the "one best way" to perform
particular tasks. Workers then could be trained or programmed, so to say,
to perform these optimal routines, and supervisors would have objective
operational standards against which to hold workers accountable.

Because workers' cooperation in these undertakings could not simply
be assumed or easily compelled, Taylor proposed that they be provided
with suitable working conditions and offered individual incentives in the
shape of proper pay for performance. (He believed, in fact, that workers'
interests, at base, were the same as were their bosses—i.e., prosperity—and
that all boats would rise together on that tide.)

Taylor insisted that work be "fully planned out," and that staffs of specialized planners (rather than line managers) do it. The planner's job was to define in detail the tasks to be done in an enterprise: what is to be done and how. Their "scientific" analyses would yield value- or interest-free specifications of task-performance requirements that would form a basis for scientific selection of suitable workers and for specifying their training requirements. Furthermore, the same analyses could be expected to yield fair and impersonal standards for deciding workers' output requirements —that is, "a proper day's work." (This Taylorist planning requirement, along with its emphasis on specialization and hierarchic control of work became universalized managerial principles in the hands of the so-called Classical Management School [Fayol, Gulick, Urwick, Drucker, et al.; see Drucker, 1974], whose formulations, unlike Taylor's, also elevated the principle of "unity of command" to a sacred station.)

Regarding the scientific analysis, standardization, and mechanization of task performance about which we have been speaking, Taylor saw these as necessitating that work in the shop (although not in the offices) be made as simple as possible. Work assignments, he thought, should be specialized, in the interest of effective skill development by large numbers of workers, and also to make their supervision easier. Supervisors, of course, had themselves to be specialized with respect to the work they oversaw and were expected to control. Hence, a consistent division of labor between workers and managers had to be maintained, in order to ensure that all work was done in accord with its plan.

Taylor's requirement for task-based specialization encouraged him in a view of organizations as complex functional networks characterized not by one but by many lines of authority, each one rationally based on the expertise basic to particular tasks. This Taylorist image of the now-familiar functional organization came with a view of the manager not as a commander so much as a servant of the worker, a specialized professional whose job it is to help the worker and ensure suitable conditions for the performance of that worker's tasks. The functional operating system, in its turn, was to be supported by a staff of technical specialists whose jobs were not necessarily to assist in doing the organization's work, but rather to define that work, its methods of performance, and the standards for its evaluation. Specialized staff also were required to select and train those who would do the work according to the specifications of the planners and designers.

The Technostructure of the Modern Organization

It was to this phenomenon of specialized technical staff that Galbraith (1967) referred when he spoke of the "technostructure" of the New Industrial

State, and suggested that, in the modern organization, "it is not the managers who decide. Effective power is lodged deeply in the technical, planning, and other specialized staff" (p. 69). Much like Taylor, Galbraith likened this technostructure to "the brain" of the modern enterprise. However, what Taylor saw as vital to the productivity of the enterprise (i.e., the development of technical planning and control staffs), Galbraith saw as at least a potential threat to it, should the so-called professional aims of these elements prove materially different from those of the enterprise, as he thought they might.

Taylor saw the ideas of scientific management as "revolutionary," involving, as they did, "a shift of emphasis from division of surplus to increasing the size of the surplus until it is so large nobody quarrels over its division" (1947, p. 61). Taylor saw himself as a "benefactor" of the species, for under scientific management, *everybody* would be better off. Ironically, however, "Taylorism" has been more a term of opprobrium than of honor. Still, the developments it signifies—the purposeful systematic rational modernization of society—have been no less revolutionary for having been gradual or less stressful for having been inevitable.

Their culmination (to date, at any rate) is the formalized phenomenon of the detached, prescriptive, organizational technostructure that epitomizes the modern work organization. There, as Henry Mintzberg (1979) describes it, "are the analysts concerned with adaptation, with changing the organization to meet environmental change, and those concerned with control, with stabilizing and standardizing patterns of activity in the organization" (p. 30). It is precisely the technostructure's environmentally sensitive adaptive role that establishes it as a key mediator between the local organization and the external social forces that impinge on it. At the same time, in its panorganizational technical nature and affiliations, an organization's technostructure imports those same societal influences into the local organization. Thus professionalized technostructures (planners, analysts, designers, personnel managers, and trainers) act not as buffers against change, but as facilitators of it—as agents working to rationalize (to modernize)—local organizations, not excluding the police.

MODERNIZATION OF POLICE AGENCIES

It is, of course, only in the larger American police departments, in some state police agencies, and certainly such organizations as the Federal Bureau of Investigation (FBI) that one is apt to find distinct technostructural elements of the sort described by Galbraith and Mintzberg (planning and analysis bureaus, training units, research and development offices). However, the modern rationalizing influences signaled by the phenomenon of the organizational technostructure are a general contextual influence on police everywhere in America. (Actually, in certain respects, the FBI, via its academy and its technical services, plays a kind of technostructural role in the law enforcement industry and hence is an important, if perhaps not deliberate, modernizing agent for the American police in general.)

The institutions and organizations of society are of a piece, more or less. We must be careful not to exaggerate the homogeneity of societies, but some degree of homogeneity is essential to their integrity and cohesion, to their distinctiveness, to their existence, in fact. It is this distinctiveness of societies that is caught by the idea of culture. The police are elements within societies and cultures. They can be expected to reflect the general norms, themes, and institutional tensions of the societies and cultures within which they operate. We refer more than once in this book to the culture of policing. In the next chapter, we begin an analysis of the ways in which the institutional forces of modernization have affected policing.

4

Modernization of the American Police

In one degree or another, modernization is a fact for policing and police agencies, just as it is everywhere else in the United States. "A conjunction of structural, situational, and personal factors . . . 'produced' the police as we know them" (Manning, 1977, p. 38)—a distinctive institution, however, sui generis, Bouza (1990) claims (with some exaggeration), atomized into thousands of locally autonomous agencies, while the rest of the world "went national." Because of its remarkably decentralized and local nature, the modernization of the police in America has inevitably been uneven and remains far from complete.

On the one hand, therefore, the police "as we know them" are products of modernizing forces; and the social forces that produced them continue to change them, in some ways greatly. At the same time, in other ways, modernization of the police remains rudimentary in America—more apparent and rhetorical than real. Unresolved tensions and discontents of modernization still are being played out in the world of American policing, and police chiefs naturally are at the center of many, maybe most, of the conflicts generated by the process.

POLICE IN AMERICA

Public police forces, after all, are relatively recent in America. Into the mid-nineteenth century, policing in U.S. cities was the province of the night watchman. American communities drew on a traditional nonintrusive English model of policing, which relied chiefly on private individuals, thief-catching firms, and a loose network of constables, watchmen, and courts for maintaining order (Moore & Kelling, 1983).

By 1829, however, the growth of cities, crime, and riots prompted the Metropolitan Police Act in England, which led to the patrolling of London by the Metropolitan Police, a full-time, uniformed, civil police force with a military hierarchy (and a detective branch). In 1845, following this English model, New York City organized the first modern American police department with a centralized command structure. Others soon followed, first in the northeast (Boston, Philadelphia), then spreading outward to other parts of the nation. By the end of the nineteenth century, "uniformed police had become an accepted 24-hour presence" in American communities; one that had "acquired a rough-and-ready ethical code, which demanded competence and courage on the job and unswerving loyalty to one another" (Stead, 1977, p. 7) by its operatives. Along with these nineteenth-century organizational developments came certain scientific innovations (fingerprinting, criminal records maintenance) that formed a basis for a forensic science (Stead, 1977).

DEFINING THE FUNCTION
OF THE POLICE

Nineteenth-century police forces in the United States emphasized reactive patrol and continued to rely on citizens to detect crimes and on private firms for investigations (e.g., Pinkertons). As Moore and Kelling (1983) note, the functions or mandate of the nineteenth-century police were ill-defined, and their legitimacy, the source of their authority, was uncertain.

> What gave the new police force the right to interfere in private matters? Were they to be considered agents of the state, allies of current political figures, neutral instruments of the law, or specialized as professionals? In England, the police were able to draw on the traditional authority of the crown and explicit parliamentary authorization, and even so the legitimacy of the police was suspect. . . . In the United States, the police had even less on which to rely . . . so it should come as no surprise that the new police forces would be suspect and considered potentially dangerous. (Moore & Kelling, 1983, pp. 53-54)

Into the early twentieth century, in fact, despite aspirations to "depoliticize" them, urban American police forces typically were questionably allied with urban political machines. Reformers of the turn-of-century "Progressive Movement," whose numbers included Theodore Roosevelt, once head of the New York City Police Commission, advocated modernization of the police in the shape of a neutral, disciplined, bureaucratic, paramilitary organization independent of political parties. The results of their exertions rarely satisfied the hopes of the moral crusaders or those of others before and since. Certainly Roosevelt's expectations were not met. His term as Commissioner in New York "ended on a note of frustration and defeat" (Berman, 1987, p. 119).

Still, as Moore and Kelling (1983) tell the story, the spirit of progressive reform continued to evolve in the twentieth century toward a focus on serious crime rather than on maintaining order and toward movements to professionalize the police. Kelling has consistently criticized both of these trends in the belief that the loss (or abandonment) of political support and the shift away from order maintenance by the police, by "leaving an insufficient link between the aspirations and interests of local communities, and the operations of the police" (Moore & Kelling, 1983, p. 58) has, in fact, been a net debit for the police and society alike.

Turning police into professional crime-fighters is today a broadly based "police orthodoxy," as Moore and Kelling have said. Manning (1977) points out, however, in his discussion of the rise of the police and their mandate, that English reformers circa 1800 were already pressing ideas about scientific, rational, prevention-oriented police. The Peel Act of 1829 that enabled formation of the London police was itself advanced as a means toward "efficient" policing. The roots of this idea, Manning suggests, were in an early public administration model of depoliticized rational decision making, fact-based action, and administrative accountability, all of which are familiar modern bureaucratic themes.

> What was in the process of emerging [in England during the first half of the eighteenth century] was a capitalistic order relying on imperative coordination of social segments through rational-legal administration. . . . In this context "tradition" is questioned and weighed against alternative, expedient modes of government operation. (Manning, 1977, p. 81)

Nevertheless, Manning goes on to say,

> The first "bobby" who walked the streets of London could not have foreseen the present American pattern of highly organized, politically active, rationalized, mechanized, and mobile policing, nor could he have anticipated the centrality of weaponry and the direct force applied by American police. It is unlikely that he would have had much sympathy with the crime-fighting rhetoric, for at that time in London it was neither possible nor very wise to seek out criminals and attempt to combat them. The aim was more limited, simply to protect citizens and their property. (pp. 82-83)

Manning (1977) also observes, though, that "the transformation of the police mandate, forged from political reform aimed to forestall and control a massive social revolution already under way [eventually led to] the present American pattern of police work" (p. 32). On the emergence of modernized professional American police departments in today's America, Manning adds that

> Police professionalism cannot be easily separated from the bureaucratic ideal epitomized in modern police practice. . . . [The] bureaucratic commitment is designed to obviate or replace commitments to competing [particularistic] norms, such as obligations to friends, kin, or members of the same racial or ethnic group. . . . The strategies employed by the police to manage their public appearances develop from their adaptations of the bureaucratic ideal. These strategies incorporate the utilization of technology and official statistics in law enforcement, styles of patrol that attempt to accommodate the community's desire for public order with the police department's preoccupation with bureaucratic procedures, secrecy as a means of controlling the public's response to their operations, collaboration with criminal elements to foster the appearance of a smoothly run, law abiding community, and a symbiotic relationship with the criminal justice system that minimizes public knowledge of police flaws. (p. 128)

Manning's sketch of police bureaucracy obviously is not one of uniform rational-legal character. As was said, against this organizational and normative criterion, police modernization in America must be judged incomplete. So it is. American policing is very much an institution in the process of becoming. Its "adaptations," as Manning calls them, of the bureaucratic norm reflect self-shaping accommodations to its formative history, its current interests, and the surrounding conditions of its existence, which are the subjects of the remainder of this book.

5

Politics and the Police Chief

Progressive reform and modernization of the police have had as a consistent primary objective the depoliticization of the police and their conversion to rational, professional norms of conduct. An implied antinomy of *political* and *professional,* therefore, pervades much of the rhetoric on modernization. The police and their leaders are inescapably political, however, especially in their localized American form.

In *The Police Mystique* (1990), a book widely admired in progressive police circles, Tony Bouza observes that "the chief's selection is a political act, and virtually everything the chief undertakes can have political implications" (p. 42). Yet, the jacket blurb for the book quotes Donald Fraser, the Mayor of Minneapolis, where Bouza served as chief until his retirement a few years ago, praising Bouza for having "pulled our police department out of politics and restored its professionalism."

Fraser plainly has in mind a sordid kind of "politics": partisan, self-seeking, petty, Machiavellian, and above all, corrupt—the kind of politics familiarly associated with greedy, power-hungry and graft-ridden big-city machines that exploit the instruments of government, including the police, for narrowly selfish purposes. Bouza recognizes this seamy kind of politics, of course—he is an intellectual man, but, after nearly 40 years of police experience in New York City and Minneapolis, hardly an innocent one. In the preceding quotation, he is referring to a broader, more descriptive, and less brazen sort of politics, one that, as he puts it, has simply to do with "the complex of forces at work around [the chief]" (p. 230). His book is filled with illustrations of these forces, their sources, and their local manifestations, all of which are neatly summarized in this passage:

> A chief's daily fare is composed of town hall meetings or angry citizens demanding action, foaming editorials, decrying an action or a failure to act, a nervous mayor's insistent summons, a council's brutal cross-examination, or calls and letters from disaffected citizens. (p. 80)

Add to this the unions, other employee groups, state government officials and functionaries, plus the many, many other interested parties of all sorts with which a chief must deal, and it is easy to see why police chiefs, especially in major cities, come to feel themselves in a storm at sea aboard a leaking and rudderless ship with a mutinous crew. More than a few of them run into political trouble and lose their jobs simply because they do not understand the nature of those jobs and the forces that bear on them (Neilsen, 1990).

POLICE ORGANIZATIONS
AND THEIR ENVIRONMENTS

As public organizations (or "bureaus" or "bureaucracies"), police depart-ments, in the language of social science, are specialized and formalized agencies of the state, operating within a legitimized charter (about which we offer more discussion later). Police departments, of course, are public organizations located within larger governmental systems. Decisions and actions by police agencies, whether in policy or operational areas, are in-fluenced by structures, procedures, and standards, not only within the police agency but also in other parts of the governmental system, too. They also are subject to both continuous and episodic influence by organized inter-ests elsewhere in the society (Gamson, 1968).

The host of different and at least potentially influential parties in an organization's institutional environment can actually be sorted into a manageable number of categories. Figure 5.1 does this for the police. The diagram depicts a network of partisans, or the "roster of actors" as we call it, available to participate in police decision making.

The arrows in the diagram are meant to suggest a potential for mutual influence among the actors in the network. Police agencies, as we said earlier, do not simply react to their environments, political or other. They may seek to and often succeed in influencing other actors. Indeed, they are intended by design to influence their clientele.

For our purposes here, the focal organization at the center of the network is the local *Police Agency (A)*. (We might speak alternatively of a focal actor, should interest concentrate on an individual chief, for instance, rather than on a police agency.) The focal organization is where the decisions and actions that interest us occur, although the agency (or chief) may not have full or final power to implement decisions in particular cases.

The category of actors called *Quasi-Publics (B)* in the diagram includes police unions, police review commissions, professional police agencies (e.g., the International Association of Chiefs of Police [IACP], the Police

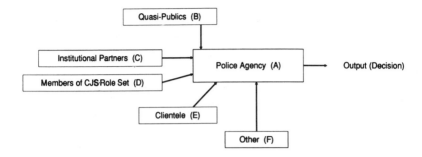

Figure 5.1. A Police Agency's Roster of Actors

Foundation) and the like. All of these are variably powerful actors closely linked to organized police work, but they are outside any particular police agency and are not components of the criminal justice system itself.

Institutional Partners (C) include relevant actors in the governmental system that controls budgeting (at least) for some particular police agency (e.g., mayors, city managers, city councils, and possibly certain others such as state or federal agencies that fund specific police programs). Institutional partners are especially important actors in the local police agency's network because they have direct and formally legitimized means of affecting those agencies. Bouza, in fact, calls mayors "the most important person[s] in law enforcement" (p. 44). They frequently hold the power of the purse and of appointment, together with its flip side, dismissal:

> The American police chief who is responsible to a politically elected official comes close to the position of "patrimonial bureaucrat" in Weber's terms. His tenure as chief, though not necessarily his tenure in the department, depends on continuing acceptability to the elected official(s). (Bordua & Reiss, 1966, p. 74)

Chiefs, therefore, often find themselves in the middle of local political infighting and electoral wrangles over the outcomes or even the terms of which they have little real control. During 1992, in Houston, for example, Elizabeth Watson, the only woman at the head of a major U.S. police department, was fired by a newly elected mayor who had campaigned on promises of tougher law enforcement. According to a report in the *New York Times* (February 15, 1992, p. A20), Watson had had some "public relations problems, but no major crises" during her roughly 2 years as chief. The new mayor, however, in announcing her removal, said that "the new administration would be better off with a new police chief and break rather clean with whatever may have been the problems in the past whether they were Chief Watson's making or not."

Meanwhile, what we term the *CJS Role Set (D)* encompasses other actors in the criminal justice system (CJS). These include *counterpart agencies* (i.e., other police departments), *interface agencies* (courts, prosecutor offices, etc.), and *support services* (e.g., central police laboratories or data processing services).

The *Clientele (E)* of a police department includes a melange of citizens, public interest groups (lobbies), political organizations, and, yes, at least potentially, offenders, too. The influence of clients on local police agencies may sometimes be direct—when they are organized, for instance, or are celebrities, such as Zsa-Zsa Gabor—but it is more likely to be indirect and symbolic. So-called community-oriented policing, interestingly, is a style of policing nominally oriented toward empowering clients by orienting police efforts toward meeting the clients' requirements (see Couper & Lobitz, 1991a). (We say more about this movement later in the book.)

Finally, *Other (F)* actors encompass a miscellany of partisans (or information sources) acting at the local level (e.g., computer salespeople, university/college instructors of management science or police science courses, reporters, police informers, and even inanimate actors such as newspapers (see Gates, 1992, on the influence of informants on police operations, and for extended discussion of one chief's view of the media and its influence). This category also comprises actors more remote from the local police department (e.g., national magazines, professional periodicals, and state-level office holders, who might, however, also act as clients or agents of clients, in which cases they might be classified as clients).

The many interested and partisan actors around a particular police department could be differently classified, perhaps, but the diagram provides a serviceable orientation to the scope and variety of partisan interests that constitute a local police department's political milieu. What the diagram only weakly conveys, however, is the dynamic quality of this milieu. Depending on conditions, partisanship may vary in its forms (e.g., it may be expressed directly or indirectly), in its intensity, in its frequency, and in the ways of its expression both within and among the several categories of actors in the model. Hence, the network is necessarily changeable, unstable, even volatile, altering its characteristics with time and circumstances. Today's coalition of the chief and a city council in opposition to a mayor's efforts to centralize precincts may dissolve tomorrow in the tempers of controversy over an alleged act of police brutality.

Further compounding the complexity of a police chief's world is the always shifting distribution of interests within the department itself. Everyone there is both an actor and a partisan. Broad and issue-specific coalitions of interests emerge and sometimes, as with unions, become institutionalized, and, in any case, often involve connections with external actors. It may be, as Bouza says, that the police chief's task "is to see to the people's interests and to keep working to promote them" (p. 187). However, it is easy to see why many chiefs fail to do this, even when they want to. All the noise, confusion, and pressures surrounding the chiefs make it hard for them to discern where the public's interests lie and harder still to see how those interests are to be promoted.

POLICE CHIEFS AS POLITICAL ACTORS

Equating politics with partisan interests, police work, as Bouza maintains, is inherently political. In recognition of the fact, the IACP, with financial support from the NEC Corporation, has recently established a Police Leadership Institute. Announcing this development in an editorial in *The Police Chief* (official organ of the IACP; February, 1991, p. 6), Lee Brown, then president of the association (and New York City police chief), described the institute's mission as "selecting and developing the individuals whose ethical exercise of influence over their own organizations, as well as their social and political environment, will set the standards for police leadership of the '90s." The institute will provide training, mentoring, and recognition to enhance police leadership "beyond the organization to the media, the community, the political arena, and the law enforcement network as a whole"—in short, to help police chiefs become more astute in managing the rosters of actors that define their political environments.

Of course, the police chief's position has long been recognized as being political. Police reform movements beginning in the late nineteenth century and even earlier recognized this fact, and as we discussed in Chapter 4, sought in various ways to change it. O. W. Wilson, the protégé of the commonly acclaimed father of modern American policing, August Vollmer, has himself been described as having "brought to American policing [in the 1920s and 1930s] an understanding that police work takes place in an atmosphere of conflict that is expressed through community politics" (Carte & Carte, 1977). J. Q. Wilson (1968), while noting that "deliberate community choices rarely [had] more than a limited effect on police behavior" (p. 226), nevertheless emphasized that "police work is carried out under the influence of a political culture" (p. 233); and he advised that the "police are keenly sensitive to their political environment [albeit perhaps] without being [literally] governed by it" (p. 230).

The political environment to which Wilson refers in these passages is local and adversarial. The new institutional politics of policing, which is our main concern, is more general and fundamental but harder to document rigorously. It tends to be obscured by the particularistic (and often

distractingly fascinating) overlays of traditional interest politics that pervade
its local manifestations.

The Watson case in Houston illustrates this. In fact, Watson had been
having difficulties with the previous mayor (Kathryn Whitmire), who had
appointed her, and also with the City Council. According to the *New York
Times,* Watson was "an avid proponent" of a "community-oriented" strategy of policing that had been introduced by her predecessor, Lee Brown,
before he moved to New York City as Police Commissioner. This set her
against local police groups and outside factions in her department's institutional network, which criticized the community-oriented strategy for, it was
said, slowing response times and "otherwise diluting police effectiveness."

Watson remained a staunch advocate of community-oriented policing,
but she obviously lost face as a crime-fighter at a time and in a place where
that was a serious matter. Part of Watson's problem, then, arose from the
inherent consequences of challenging established interests by playing the
role of an institutional change agent striving, in this instance, to recast the
role of the police in her community. At the same time, however, there can
be no doubt that the previous mayor's (Whitmire's) discontentment with
Watson was fueled by Watson's putting her in a position where management of the police department became a local campaign issue—and, the
Times reports, as one of her last acts as mayor, Whitmire underscored the
point by denying Watson a merit pay raise.

Such episodes as this one repeat themselves with regularity in cities
throughout the country. (We describe some others in greater detail later on.)
What makes them inevitable is not the naïveté or stupidity of individual
chiefs (although some of them are certainly naïve or stupid or both). Rather,
it is that, wittingly or unwittingly, they are inevitably either instruments
of institutional change (as Chief Watson was in Houston, and Chief Brown
was before her), or active defenders of a passing institutional status quo
(such as Chief Daryl Gates in Los Angeles).

Two quotations from a police management expert with the Labor Management Service of the U.S. Council of Mayors convey the contentious locali-
zation and particularization of the police chief's broader function as institutional change agent.

It is understandable that in many cities the police chiefs are exceedingly un-
popular with their own officers—for they must fulfill the orders of mayors and
city councils to reorganize and cut back police departments. Often they are
hired away from other cities because they gained their reputations for their administrative abilities and because as outsiders they can look more objectively
at a police department's traditional procedures than someone who came up
through the ranks.

The writer went on to observe that now, unsurprisingly, "there is a demand for police chiefs who are more administrators than cops." In the next chapter we examine this idea of the police chief as manager and consider both its operational implications and its feasibility.

6

The Police Chief as Manager

Late in his book, *Commissioner,* Murphy (1977) nominates both the top
and the bottom of police departments as the places where most of the
problems are. The problems he identifies are mainly those of accountability
and leadership. Because of this, he thinks that the problems at the top (i.e.,
mismanagement) are worse than those at the bottom. His remedy, however,
is not at all suggestive of Lone Ranger tactics. The solutions to the problems
of policing, Murphy thinks, are not to be found in masked champions on
white horses or in silver bullets. This is because the problems are considered to be technical ones (i.e., mismanagement). Presumably, then, the real
solutions to what are considered the big problems of policing will result
from putting police chiefs in "gray flannel suits"—training them to be better
administrators and equipping them with the concepts and techniques of
modern management—that is, professionalizing the police.

Quite apart from practical utility—indeed, regardless of it—modern
Western institutions are thoroughly rationalized; and modern organizations,
including police departments, therefore, stand in the thrall of general norms
of rationality (see Kieser, 1989, for discussion of these ideas in a particu-
larly apt connection, namely the transition of medieval guilds to modern
forms of enterprise). Thompson (1967), for one, has described the bureaucratization of modern societies as a hegemonic triumph of rational values.

Built into organizations and personalities, these values serve as the
taken-for-granted groundings of organizational legitimacy. In ironic consequence, rationalized structures require certain (bureaucratic) features
not by rational calculation, but simply because they are the ways that things
are done. Thus, Murphy's (and others') managerial admonitions to the
police, in effect, give voice to an institutional mythology, as Meyer and
Rowan (1977) would say, in terms of which their contemporary organizational structures and administrative practices are to be legitimized—a mythology, however, that we find at some variance with police custom.

BUREAUCRATIZING THE POLICE

"The transition [in the late nineteenth century] from the prevailing perspective of the police as an adjunct of the [local political] machine to a model of a disinterested, non-partisan and efficient agency of municipal government" was an ideological accomplishment that brought American policing under a professional model (Berman, 1987, p. 121). Monkkonen (1981) ranks so-called progressive reform, by changing control relations, bureaucratizing, and rationalizing the operations of the uniformed police, as one of two great transformations of American policing. (The first was roughly a half-century earlier, when the urban police were homogenized, put into uniforms, and integrated under centralized command structures, and began divesting themselves of welfare functions in order to concentrate on law enforcement.) Monkkonen (1981) points out, therefore, that putting the police into uniform in the mid-nineteenth century signaled *both* their authority and a bureaucratic basis for it.

MANAGING THE POLICE

Trust in the wisdom and feasibility of managerial solutions to police problems has thus been visibly gathering in America since at least the late nineteenth century. It has been pushed in one or another way by such notables as Teddy Roosevelt, August Vollmer, Orville Wilson; by numerous blue ribbon committees; and by frequent governmental commissions. The idea now is all but taken for granted, and the president of the IACP, Lee Brown, has happily observed that now "outstanding management training for police organizations is readily available" (1991, p. 6).

Indeed, issues of *The Police Chief* are filled with articles on "Applied Behavioral Sciences: Training to Revitalize the First-Line Supervisor"; "Effective Followership"; "Developing a Participatory Decision-Making Model"; "Defining the Police Mission." The article by Couper and Lobitz (1991a) that was mentioned earlier describes a transformation of the ideas of problem/ community-oriented policing into the foundation of a program of TQM, titled, "The Customer Is Always Right." (We discuss Couper and Lobitz's description of the Madison programs in more detail in the second part of this book.)

A recent product of the Management Science Unit of the FBI Academy (Witham & Watson, undated) exemplifies the current state of things. Reporting on "The Role of the Law Enforcement Executive," the authors reviewed some general social science ideas on roles and then summarized Mintzberg's ideas on the nature of (business) managers' work (plus Drucker's distinction between "managers" and "executives"). They followed this with a broadly stated outline of police executive functions—diplomat-liaison, coordination, and so forth—none of which is in any way police-specific!

POLICE WORK

An equation of police chief and general manager doubtless has a certain real utility: Management, after all, is a responsibility of police chiefs, and a variety of managerial techniques can be helpful to them; but skepticism about any literal equation of police chief and CEO is called for. It seems dubious to propose that police work is just like other work, police organizations just like factories or social security offices, and police management just like managing automobile dealerships.

The Police Role:
Social Control and Force

There is no objective function of police work, only a variety of models. A contemporary consensus on the police role in (North American) society has, however, emerged around social control perspectives and the centrality of force in its definition. Taking a cue from Bittner (1970), Manning (1977), for example, described the police as social agents "that stand ready to employ force upon the citizenry on the basis of situationally defined exigencies" (p. 40). Meanwhile, Rumbaut and Bittner (1979) have emphasized projections of police power in the form of a "capacity and authority to overpower resistance."

Muir (1977), in his Weberian analysis of the police as street corner politicians, has sounded a defensive counterpoint to Manning's and Bittner's aggressive theme. For Muir, the police stand individually and collectively in a defensive posture vis-à-vis the citizenry, one induced by anticipation of the resistance they are empowered to overcome. Consequently, they are absorbed by "the cares of self-defense" (Muir, 1977, p. 5), to the point where a central part of police work is constant watchfulness for critical incidents and rebellions.

The foregoing is essentially an order-maintenance interpretation of the police function. As Wilson (1968), for one, has noted, however, there are other styles of policing, which may be considered to be either competing (normative) definitions of the police role or ancillary (empirical) features of police behavior. That is, service delivery or law enforcement activities may be identified in police performance whether or not these ideas are assumed as alternative theories of police function.[1] The point in any case is that, if in practice the police may be functionally heterogeneous, coercion is nonetheless basic to their societal role. The police are, as Bittner (1990) nicely put it, "the or else of society."

Police Work and Its Operational Context

In addition to its emphasis on force and violence (and Muir's important complementary emphasis on the fear or anticipation of resistance), Manning's and Bittner's view of the police as respondents to "situationally defined exigencies" highlights the contextual relativity and ad hoc nature of police work. With a pervading obligation to employ violence in the interests of social control, police work constitutes the application of a mixture of standard and nonstandard skills and techniques to the management of problematic social situations, many of them arising from an implicit police mandate to keep society's underclass invisible (Bouza, 1990). It is the responsibility, and prerogative, of the individual police officer, then, to interpret these commonly ambiguous situations, and to select appropriate means of handling them.

A general order on the use of force for one mid-American city's police department nicely portrays the essential discretionary nature of police action. After nearly three pages of single-spaced statements on definitions, levels, alternatives, and circumstances of deadly force, this statement appears:

> The above should NOT be construed to suggest that you should ever relax and lose control of a situation, thus endangering your personal safety or the safety of others. *Officers are permitted to use that force which is reasonable and necessary to protect themselves from bodily harm.* (emphasis in original)

Fundamental to an understanding of police behavior and organization is appreciation of the driving force of the inherently uncertain, ad hoc, and hence discretionary nature of police work—that is, the extent to which it consists of problem-solving in ambiguous and at least potentially dangerous situations.

The Organizational Context of Police Work

Police work today is organized mainly in what have been termed *commonweal organizations,* that is, organizations (many of which are quite small, two or three people) supported by public funds and granted special privileges to act in the public interest. Structured after the nineteenth-century "Peelian" model of a civil police with a military hierarchy, police operatives are unlike soldiers, however, in that they are conceived not as servants of government, but of law and so "cannot plead that [they] acted under orders from a superior" but must accept responsibility for their actions (Stead, 1977, p. 4).

Research on the nature, organization, and control of police work is "still very thin," partly, as Bouza suggests, because of police disinclination toward participating in research and their penchant toward secrecy. However, J. Q. Wilson (1968) for one has highlighted a striking feature of police organizations—namely, the fact that as one moves *down* their administrative hierarchy, discretion in decision making and action *increases*. For police departments and their chiefs, this discretionary inversion of the normal organizational pattern is an important problem in several respects. Not the least of them is sustaining democratic control of police behavior on the street. Another is maintaining its subjugation to rational standards.

The fact that violence and danger, whether actuarially frequent or not, is an omnipresent aspect of police work intensifies the problems of technical uncertainty: The perils of police work introduce a moral consideration, the safety of police officers, which can be set against the idea of limiting their discretion in handling hard-to-predict concrete cases (as in the just-described use-of-force policy). Police chiefs are, therefore, careful to avoid even the appearance of "undermining the protection" of their officers (Hunt, 1988); and the same considerations impel strong opposition by police operatives to any attempt at regulating their actions, especially attempts by outsiders, as, for instance, by citizen review boards, which police chiefs are expected by their troops to oppose on principle. (We have reported [Hunt & Magenau, 1983b], for example, how one mayor's effort to form such a citizen's committee for police oversight was derailed by his police chief's professional objections to the city council that such a body would infringe on his authority.)

The combination of uncertainty and threat in police work provides a politically useful rationale for police self-determination of the policies and methods—the norms—by which they operate. In one city we studied, for example, opposition (including strike threats) by police officers to the installation of computer terminals in patrol cars was based mainly on their beliefs about the equipment's potential for enabling increased external supervision and control of their activities. (This was, indeed, an administrative advantage of the terminals, but opposition nevertheless cooled as officers discovered ways of using the terminals for their own ends, e.g., to have off-the-[audio] record conversations with colleagues.)

Meyer and Rowan (1977) have argued cogently that myths of institutional environments shape organizational structures more powerfully than do the demands of work activities. Perhaps so; but the blunt fact remains that discretion is an *inherent* property of police work, and police organization perforce reflects the constraining influence of the work itself. As Morris Janowitz (1961) has pointed out,

> the military establishment with its hierarchical structure, with its exacting requirements for coordination, and with its apparently high centralization of organizational power, must strive contrariwise to develop the broadest decentralization of initiative at the point of contact with the enemy. (p. 210)

He goes on to say that

> The combat soldier . . . when committed to battle, is hardly the model of Max Weber's ideal bureaucrat following rigid rules and regulations. . . . Rather his role is one of constant improvisation. (p. 210)

Similar to the work of the combat soldier, police work requires officers

> not only to count on instruction from superiors, but also to exercise their own judgment about the best responses to make when confronted with danger. (p. 211)

Unlike the combat soldier, however, the police officer on the street deals with ambiguity not only episodically when confronted with danger in battle, but routinely. The essence of the process of arrest, J. Q. Wilson (1989) notes, is judgment. Situations and the people in them are not all alike, and cops on the street must decide spontaneously how (and whether) they will deal with them. As street-level bureaucrats, individual police officers manufacture the rules they will enforce and must adapt or ignore the ones that are manufactured for them, depending on how they perceive their interests and situations.

In any case, "it is very difficult," Wilson suggests, "to specify by rule in advance who should be stopped [on the street], questioned, or searched." Consequently, police tend to be cautious and even underenforce the law (because of expectations of after-the-fact political criticism). Rules that might tell officers who they may stop, when, and what they can do are apt to be "cumbersome, incomplete, and even inconsistent." For reasons of their own, then, some cops will ignore or evade rules such as these, while others, "determined to stay out of trouble, will use the rules as an excuse for doing as little as possible" (p. 328). What is more, because police work does not always "leave a paper trail," police officers are "relatively free to use their discretion" (p. 41), and of course they do.

Neither legislatures nor police administrators can dominate patrol officers, Wilson has observed, and for the same reason—the nature of the

work. The intrinsically discretionary nature of that work greatly complicates the organization and control of the work and of its practitioners.

NOTE

1. In a review of the literature on what the police do, Wycoff (1982) found that, in
many cases, officers spent less than 30% of their time doing things that could be thought
of as directly related to law enforcement. The rest of their time was distributed over a
variety of order maintenance, service, traffic, and other activities. The proportion of time
spent on law-enforcement activity, however, tended to vary with jurisdiction: from a low of
7% of patrol time in a "small town" to a high of 52% in one New York City precinct.

7

The Institutional Context of Police Organization

Once developmentally past the free-form individual constable operating under an open-ended peacekeeping, order-maintenance charter, traditional police organization is basically along the lines of a craft. As Mintzberg (1979) describes it, a *craft-based structure* is informally organized around the skills of operators. Neither its work products nor its processes are standardized. Its division of labor, based on craft skills that are acquired and standardized via apprenticeship training, is not rigid. Jobs are easily interchanged, and interdependencies are handled via mutual adjustments rather than by formal rules. Hence, in a craft organization, there is *little need for direct supervision* or for a recognized leader. If there is a leader, he or she is likely to work right alongside the other members of the group, doing tasks comparable to theirs, so status distinctions are modest. Consequently, the administrative component of craft organizations tends to be small and undifferentiated, with a few managers working alongside the oper- ators; because there is little standardization of work processes or outputs (as distinct from inputs, skills) in craft structures, there is little need for technostructure.

The craft organization plainly differs sharply from usual images of modern rational-legal bureaucratic systems. These "machine bureaucracies," as Mintzberg calls them, are organizational varieties that are typified by high degrees of job specialization, an elaborated hierarchy of authority, a large administrative component, close supervision, large and formalized work units, technostructural elaboration, and, of course, standardization of work outputs and processes. In the craft organization, power is a function of the individual's expertise; in the machine bureaucracy, it is a matter of the individual's office (or job).

POLICE DEPARTMENTS AS
PROFESSIONAL BUREAUCRACIES

Actual police departments, like many other functioning organizations, naturally exhibit mixtures and blendings of structural characteristics. Many of them resemble what has been called a "professional bureaucracy." This amounts to an elaborated version of craft organization in which craft characteristics are combined with machine-bureaucratic features. Unlike a machine bureaucracy, however, a professional bureaucracy operates according to standards that originate *outside* the local organization, in a trans- cendent professional or other community. Hence, instead of loyalty to the values of a particular local organization, professionals owe their principal loyalty to their profession. So it is with, police officers, who, although em- ployees of particular agencies, enjoy a common status as cops and an attachment to the professional culture or craft of policing.

Mintzberg paints a simple form of professional bureaucracy as one where trained professionals practice standard skills under the leadership of a strong, even autocratic leader. Structures such as these certainly exist in police venues, as is shown later in this book. Mintzberg also describes a "dispersed professional bureaucracy" which he illustrates with the Royal Canadian Mounted Police (RCMP). Many Mounties work alone as autonomous professionals in remote locations far from an administrative structure, with near-total discretion over their work. In cases such as the RCMP, loyalty and work standards are maintained chiefly by training and indoctrination. Operators thereby come to carry work norms and skills with them wherever they go.

The point of drawing an analogy between police officers and craftspersons is to depict them as a kind of worker (professional, perhaps) who customarily learns traditional skills through lengthy apprenticeship training and then is allowed to practice those skills largely free from direct supervision in organizations having relatively modest administrative components, no technostructure, and few managers, many of whom simply work alongside them. To be sure, modern police organizations have tended to evolve away from these traditional structures toward more bureaucratic forms, but the craft influence nevertheless persists in contemporary police organization.

THE CRAFT SKILLS OF POLICE WORK

The skills necessary for police work are complex[1] and, by and large, still are learned, formally and informally, on the job in master-apprentice and/or comparable relations. "Any time you step out of your patrol car or walk through a door, you and your partner better know what you are going to do . . . that's what they hammered into us over and over again" at the police academy (Gates, 1992, p. 44). Chief Gates also notes that experienced police officers are able to "spot all kinds of activity that an average person might not notice." An interesting example of such craft skills is the way in which a cop on the street may recognize someone carrying a concealed weapon: "Does the front edge of his jacket cling to one thigh more than the other? As he steps off the curb, does his hand brush his hip?" Such skills are also shown in how he or she may test the suspicion: "When you stop a man with a gun, 99 out of 100 times he's going to do the same thing. He's going to turn the side with the gun on away from you . . . and the hand and arm are going to come naturally in the direction of the gun, in an instinctive protective motion" (described by New York City Detective Robert T. Gallagher to the *New York Times,* May 26, 1992, p. B3).

Because of its ad hoc character, the processes of police work resist standardization and formalization and tend toward organization into organic structures (Burns & Stalker, 1966) built around the craft skills of its workers. With little administrative-managerial differentiation or elaboration in such organizational environments, there tends to be little interest in bureaucratic techniques for rational decision making, planning, policy formation, or resource allocation (Wilson, 1968). Within a customary system of shared beliefs and values on the purposes and nature of policing, mutual adjustment and assistance among workers, and (secondarily) direct supervision by craft masters (e.g., sergeants) are the primary traditional means of coordinating and controlling craft-based police work.

These circumstances call to mind descriptions of medieval guilds and their emphases on nonutilitarian values, membership rules, honor, the maintenance of solidarity, and the importance to them of symbol, myth, and ceremony (see Kieser, 1989). The guilds, in Kieser's account, were a predecessor institution of the modern rationalized organization. In an evolutionary struggle, they ultimately collapsed in the face of competition from more efficient economically rational "putting-out systems," as Kieser calls more formal bureaucratic structures. As for police departments:

It is only somewhat exaggerated to compare modern American police departments with the manorial fiefdoms of Europe in the Middle Ages. The central figure of the local chief looms uncommonly large in the highly decentralized context of U.S. policing. The quasi-military command structure, customs of obedience to the chief, and traditions of reciprocal loyalty encourage an analogy between police organizations and feudal systems of vassalage. The point is that police agencies in the [United States] exhibit concentration of power but in a framework of still more powerful local custom. This marks the character even of the 17,000 or so modern-day metropolitan police agencies in the [United States]. The power of the local chief is *within* a system. It does not include a license to change that system, quite the opposite. (Hunt, 1987, pp. 15-16)

Thus in the contemporary American police department, it is possible to perceive a still incomplete transition where the struggle between custom and rationalist modernization continues.

BUREAUCRATIZING AND PROFESSIONALIZING THE POLICE

In a context of institutional pressures toward rationalization, growth in the size and scope of metropolitan police organizations has combined with internal managerial and external political/reform interests in regulating police activities and restricting working-level discretion. This has impelled the two often-competing modern developments we have been discussing —namely, the bureaucratization and the professionalization of police work (see, Monkkonen, 1981; Walker, 1983, 1985). These countervailing tendencies can be read as reflecting the inevitable and perhaps uneven contest posited by Meyer and Rowan (1977) between the production systems of organizations, on the one side, and their institutional environment, on the other. The craftlike nature of police work—its production system—pulls its structures toward some decentralized variety of professionalization at the same time that institutional norms of rationality are pulling toward efficiently centralized bureaucratic forms. The police department as a professional bureaucracy, represents, then, an intermediate form of police organization that remains in continuous structural tension as it seeks an accommodation to stubbornly contrary internal and external organizing pressures.

Professionalizing the Police

By custom, professions claim broad legal, moral, and intellectual mandates to define their work (Hughes, 1959). They may themselves define the norms of proper conduct and suitable modes of belief for and about themselves. Accession to professional status is tantamount to a license to practice —a grant of operational discretion from society. However, this discretion is within a range of moral, intellectual, and practical conditions. Professionalization, in one sense, liberates its members for practice, but, in another sense, it represents an instrument of societal control. It insulates practitioners from detailed community influence while providing a mechanism of regulation via standards of entry and practice. If not an altogether far-fetched idea, professionalism in this formal sense probably has almost no real current bearing on the police case, except perhaps in marginal and symbolic ways.

DeCottis and Kochan (1978) have said flat out that the patrol officer is not a professional. Their test for such status is that (a) a job be specialized at the occupational rather than at the individual or organizational level, (b) emphasis on job performance be on its process rather than on its product, and (c) it be informed by a unique, codified body of occupational knowledge. The contemporary emphasis on professionalization among the police, however, has affected their training, organizational structures, entrance requirements, and other factors of their employment, such that they now occupy a marginal status somewhere between professional and non- professional (DeCottis & Kochan, 1978).

Still, as Stead (1977) has said, no doubt correctly, "the best people in any occupation take a professional view of their work, in the sense that they do it ably, wholeheartedly, with keen awareness of their duty and in a spirit of service" (p. 8). As our foregoing discussion suggested, professionalization is a more or less natural elaboration of the craft system that occurs when work skills become encoded into a formalized body of knowledge. As a preliminary to practice, the knowledge and skill then can be acquired via formal education and/or training, instead of by an apprenticeship system. Like craftspersons, professionals retain high levels of individual discretion in deciding on the actual performance of their skills. Regulation of professional conduct, and hence limitation of professional discretion, is accomplished essentially by the standardization of skills, buttressed by such provisions as certification, licensing, and general oversight to monitor compliance with both technical and moral norms of professional practice.

An example of this from our studies of decision making in police organizations (Magenau & Hunt, 1989) occurred in a West Coast city, which had adopted a new policy intended to limit police use of lethal force. By defi- nition, *policy* represents an attempt at standardizing performance by bringing it under external normative control. In this case, an additional step was taken beyond the simple promulgation of policy. A deliberate attempt was made to institutionalize the policy via development of a computerized shoot/do-not-shoot simulator to support intensive police officer training to ensure that they shoot according to policy.

Effective professionalization of the police (or any other occupation), however, requires more than formalization of a body of technical knowledge. It requires, too, a taxonomy of situations (pigeonholes that signal

who is to be treated how) according to which allocational decisions may be
made regarding methods of their standard operational treatment. Wilson's
(1968) differentiation of service, law enforcement, and order maintenance
functions for police, and the implied differentiation of techniques appropriate to their performance, gets to this diagnostic point, but their vague-
ness testifies to the modest level of police professionalization (although,
in truth, classification systems, even in medicine, commonly are vague
and judgmental).

Bureaucratization of the Police Role

In its 1967 report, the Task Force on the Police of the President's Commission on Law Enforcement and Administration of Justice observed that
"America is a nation of small, decentralized police forces" (p. 3). So it still
is; but, as we have seen, change, of a kind, has been appearing in this scene.
The recommendations of the Task Force were themselves an indicator and
an institutional statement of it. They proposed no merger of police forces
into national or regional constabularies, but they did envisage holding
American policing to universal standards, common policies, and model
structures. This marked a shift of emphasis toward at least implicitly
centralized contractual or quasi-contractual regulation of police organization and operation in the United States (see Salerno, 1981). As we
discuss later, this has been abetted by formalized labor-management
agreements (and by the training activities of the FBI Academy and
organizations such as the IACP).

With the continuing elaboration of police-agency functions in formal
organizations, institutional pressures have steadily increased to bring those
organizations and functions under an instrumentally rational model of
police work focused on standardizing its outputs as well as its inputs (see
Monkkonen, 1981, for a discussion in historical context). Plainly, such
modeling requires some sort of invariant definition of what the outputs of
police work are, of what it is the police are supposed to produce. Also plainly,
this is difficult to specify, given the complex character of police work. To
some extent, however, it has been accomplished by a narrowed model of
police work specifically as law enforcement. This, as Manning observes,
is a relatively "recent development that has [defined] the police as an ap-
pendage of the law rather than as an extension of the violence potential
of the state" (1977, p. 40). What it does (among other things) is to suggest
a clear (if, in Wilson's [1968] eyes, a secondary) mandate for police work
(i.e., law enforcement) and a basis for standardizing its outcomes in the shape

of even-handed law enforcement cum justice (cf. Rumbaut & Bittner, 1979).

If, in Manning's (1977) words, the law is claimed as a "fount of legitimacy," it establishes an abstract rather than some specific situational-communitarian basis of police practice—a rationalized bureaucratic instead of a contextual or customary grounding. Establishing the police as agents of the law rather than of a citizenry (or state), Manning suggests, serves "as a mystification device or canopy to cover selectively, legitimate, and rationalize police conduct" (1977, p. 101). It fuels as well a bureaucratic-managerial rationalization of police organization, which stresses its formalization, internal operational-administrative differentiation and centralization, and its conversion to instrumental-technocratic values.

All of this was part of an ambitiously grand design for modernizing the police in one large southern city. Its objective was to have a model police department. The plan for getting it revolved around the innovative use of technology: patrol cars equipped with TV monitors for video surveillance; mobile teleprinters tied into a central computer for immediate data access; street corner TV cameras; vertical patrol via helicopters; and a new computerized information system—all coordinated from an ultrasecure headquarters building housing the most sophisticated equipment available. The plan also provided for new administrative systems and for suitable person- nel development (which, incidentally, prompted reaction from the troops because the progressive chief appeared not to trust their reliability or sensitivity to community interests).

This city's example expresses the contemporary thrust toward transforming police work into a "value-free technical activity, involving the objective and expert application of science and technology in the neutral and rational interests of operational efficiency" (Rumbaut & Bittner, 1979, p. 282; see also Manning, 1983). By modernization, the city intended to accomplish a planful regulation of police work via administrative systems instead of relying on police officer judgment—an intrusion of values, masked, in effect, by hardware.

To speak of professionalization in this setting, however, is to refer not so much to individual police officers as to police institutions. The term is thus a screen or euphemism for bureaucratization of the police, which is sometimes motivated by rational administrative zeal (as in the case of an August Vollmer or an O. W. Wilson and the modernization example just described) and sometimes by hopes for policy-guided moral reform (as in the case of a Herman Goldstein [1977] problem-oriented policing, or the shoot-to-policy example mentioned earlier).

MODERN POLICE ORGANIZATION

Thus can be described the developmental tendencies of contemporary police organization toward a public form of professional bureaucracy. Implicit in the development are some pointedly conflicting themes having to do with the mandate, normative basis, and performance of police work. Conditioning the whole is the inherent complexity of police craft work (i.e., the variety of the tasks it involves, the ambiguity of situational cues available for selecting alternative tactics, and the absence of clear, consistent standards for evaluating performance), which limits severely the extent to which police work can be routinized and bureaucratized.

Even within a narrowed conceptualization of police work as law enforcement and commitment to its rationalization, there has so far been relatively little progress toward consensus about or establishment of a body of knowledge sufficient to specify a panoply of standard police skills and explicit conditions for their use. Nor is there yet the well-accepted means of imparting this knowledge to practitioners that would bring policing into any close resemblance to a profession (Sherman, 1978). The term *professional* continues to mean different things to different people, who also have different motives for supporting its application in police venues.

Sherman (1978) noted, for example, that raising the social status of police work has been a central concern of the police themselves. Hence, it is hardly surprising to learn that police organizations (unions and fraternal associations) advocate professionalization as a means of status enhancement and invoke imagery of the so-called free professions, medicine and law (Hughes, 1959). Indeed, Price (1977) maintains that historically the police invoke the "rhetoric of professionalism" whenever they fall under attack from outsiders, including reformist or managerialist chiefs, who seek to restrict their operational discretion. The rhetoric of professionalism here, then, is a defense against external control just as, in other hands, "professionalism" may be an instrument of its assertion.

What we see in police organization today is in fact an inchoate mix of bureaucratizing and professionalizing tendencies, overlaid on a traditional free-form organic pattern of ad hoc police behavior at the working level. The result, especially in larger departments, as we mentioned earlier, resembles the kinds of parallel structures common to professional bureaucracies (Mintzberg, 1979). Administrative and support staff in these departments are organized in hierarchies similar to machine bureaucracies, which are, however, only loosely coupled with a quite decentralized organization of police operations, which, furthermore, is only modestly professionalized. Hence, despite superior resources and sanctioning power, administrative influence over police operations (as distinct from staff and administrative bureaus) is tenuous and, to a large extent indirect and symbolic. It is a system, moreover, laden with tension and conflict, much of it focused on police administrators.

NOTE

1. By *complex,* we mean that police work is nonroutine. Nonstandard responses must be fashioned in situations, the meaning of which is equivocal, and under conditions where criteria for evaluating the "effectiveness" of these responses are ambiguous.

8

The Institutional Position
of the Police Administrator

The administrator is caught in the middle—without clear standards, adequate rules, reliable information, or sufficient resources. It is because he
feels caught that he is more likely to make imprudent public statements
about this matter than any other. Some chiefs try to identify with their
men by attacking (and enraging) those who fail to "support the police"
and who "stir up trouble"; others try to soothe the community, and thus
enrage their own men, by promising that they can "live" with a civilian review board. (J. Q. Wilson, 1968, pp. 74-75)

The many factors that work to limit a chief's capacity for command originate both inside and outside their departments, as we have said. Despite
rhetoric about chains of command and quasi-military structures of police
organization,[1] the ability of chiefs and other police administrators to influence the operations of their weakly rationalized bifurcated departments
is naturally quite modest, and it has been made still more so by the growth
of police unions. Needless to say, this is a source of endemic frustration alike
to progressive reform-oriented political police chiefs, like Patrick Murphy,
and modern technocratic public administration-oriented types.

Our own studies of police decision making (Hunt & Magenau, 1983a,
1983b; Magenau & Hunt, 1989) underscore the attenuated power positions
of police chiefs. They depict the numerous actors who participate in police
decisions and their contending preferences; and they reveal the many
ways in which police administrators may be caught between the interests
of the rank and file and the community. They also pointedly suggest a
power of the rank and file and their agencies to influence features of the
police role.

Every management decision we've made has had to be weighed against: how
will the unions react? Will this decision go to arbitration? Will someone file

a grievance? . . . It's a mistake to fight union organization but it's an equal mistake to make false assumptions about union-management relations in the public sector. To assume that ambiguity in union contracts will be interpreted in favor of the principle of public service or police professionalism is to fail in the recognition that the public service ideal has been greatly diminished by the realities of contemporary police management-union relationships.

This, from the executive of a department in a large urban rust-belt county where, of some 1000 members, only 3 (including himself) did not belong to a union, may depict an extreme (and somewhat self-righteously described) case; but in each of the numerous cases we have studied, the interests of the rank and file, when they were threatened, prevailed over those of other groups. This was true, for instance, in the already mentioned shooting-policy case; and it was also true when police officers in another midwestern city pressed a case for more effective weapons, specifically .357-magnum handguns. The police chief thought these quite visible weapons would inflame his (liberal) community; but a compromise eventually was worked out that involved retention of .38-caliber pistols as standard weapons, but the use in them of hollow-point ammunition (which is believed to have greater stopping power than other kinds but is less visible than bigger guns).

A similar situation developed in a West Coast city, when a police shooting produced serious community unrest. A committee of the city council convened to study the police department's weapons policy, which turned out to be quite tolerant: Officers could use almost any kind and caliber handgun they chose—and they chose a variety of them. The council recommended standardization on the common .38-caliber revolver. The chief favored this policy and also wished to appear responsive to the council. The rank and file were strongly against it, claiming that it involved matters of life and death. Negotiation of the issue resulted in standardization, however, not on the .38, but on the more powerful .357 magnum, plus grandfathering of different weapons previously carried by individual officers. Later collective bargaining added the .41-magnum revolver to the authorized list, as a sweetener, a departmental concession "to clinch the deal when it got down to the wire" (see Magenau & Hunt, 1989).

The fact, however, that a recent fad in police weaponry is the 9-mm automatic—which trades firepower for speed (and maybe accuracy)—suggests that the arguments in these cases really are less about guns than they are about symbols of police officer discretion, autonomy, and bargaining position. Also, for perspective, it might be remembered that even Teddy Roosevelt ended his term as Commissioner in New York City "on a note

48   Institutional Change in Policing

of frustration and defeat" (Berman, 1987, p. 119) when his efforts at
legalistic police reform failed to meet his expectations.

LOCAL VERSUS COSMOPOLITAN
MODELS FOR POLICING

Traditional (i.e., craft-based) police organization recognized mainly sen-
iority distinctions between and among police officers. Administrators were
comparatively few, and so were class-type status differences among police
personnel. What counted was their common status as cops. (Police fraternal or benevolent associations, for example, were and are undifferentiated
mutual benefit societies, membership in which has been open to all sworn
personnel, regardless of rank or function.) In these systems, chiefs were
understood to function internally as authoritative but unifying craftmas-
ters and externally, as the occasion required, as warrior-leader or head of
the guild, representing departmental interests to resource-controlling bod-
ies and buffering the guild from outside influences (cf. Kieser, 1989).

The chief's function on this local theory of policing was, in short, to preserve and advance customary concepts and instruments of the police role
in society and, above all, as Wilson (1968) makes plain, to "back up the men."
Whether or not a particular chief consistently or even mainly conforms
to such a bottom-up agency role model, she or he will necessarily be
intensely sensitive to the role expectations and morale of departmental
rank and file and cognizant "that heavy demands are always made on that
morale by the nature of the police role" (Wilson, 1968, p. 74).

The modern police chief, however, if not universally, is now at least widely
conceived on an external or cosmopolitan theory, the model of public
administration—that is, as an instrumentally rational manager responsible
for preserving the *public's* strategic interests and for ensuring the efficient
use of public resources to those ends. We have seen Murphy's and Bouza's
bows to this model, which conceives the police administrator less as a champion and foreign minister of the police than as a middle-level functionary,
an apparatchik of a more encompassing institutional system.

The still incomplete rationalization of police institutions, however, guar-
antees that a chief will be buffeted (more or less) by conflicting role expectations and cast into a position that is inherently political, in Wilson's
explicit adversarial sense. (Gates's [1992] autobiography is an especially
rich source of examples, as is an article by Kleinman [1979] about six cases
of no-confidence votes on police chiefs.) The administrator, as Wilson put
it, is "caught in the middle—without clear standards, adequate rules, reliable
information, or sufficient resources." Some chiefs, those leaning toward

a local model of their role (such as Daryl Gates in Los Angeles), try to identify with their people by attacking (and enraging) those who fail to support the police and who stir up trouble; others, cosmopolitans, try to soothe the community, and thus enrage their own rank and file, by promising that they can live with a civilian review board.

Most chiefs hold views of their roles somewhere between the local and cosmopolitan poles, and, moreover, commonly oscillate between them. Indeed, J. Q. Wilson suggests that they tend to develop two views of their functions, one public and one private; but chiefs today, with rare exceptions, have no clear or, at any rate, no consistent conception of their roles, an idea with which Bouza would no doubt agree.

A police chief clearly is someone who is subject to conflicting expectations and pressures imposed from without by various actors in the community and from within the agency by the rank and file. Diffusely impersonal institutional forces exacerbate the conflicts. At the center of a multifaceted struggle for power to control the police agency in both its strategic and operational aspects, the power of chiefs actually to control their departments is limited, as now has been sufficiently said.

SO WHO IS IN CHARGE?

According to Louis Mayo (1985), no one is in charge. Relative to external influence, as Wilson once proposed, the police operate within a sort of Barnardian (1938) "zone of indifference." Within a framework of externally legitimized standards, a *zone of indifference* is a loosely specified range of tolerance for discretionary administrative and operational decision making. The limits of the zone ostensibly are defined by general public policies, which the police do not themselves control, but which they certainly have an interest in and an influence on. This influence may sometimes be slight, however, as one chief discovered, to his discomfort. Rankling for some time under persistent interference by his city manager, this chief angrily demanded in a public meeting, "Will you let me run my department?" To which the city manager replied simply and bluntly, "No." [2]

Still, external political control of the police is difficult, for city managers as well as for chiefs. In the first place, as Wilson (1968) points out, in order to have a political effect, a thing must first be brought under administrative control. It never is easy in complex organizations to bring anything under administrative control, but it is especially hard to do it with order maintenance. In general, the complexity of police work and the ambiguity of police performance standards and their empirical indicators militate against it. In addition, police unions and other employee associations have demonstrated an impressive ability to sustain partisanship in political contests, to mobilize support from sympathetic public constituencies, and to establish coalitions on behalf of their interests and world views.

We mentioned earlier, for instance, one city's attempt to impose a new restrictive shooting policy on its police department. A new mayor there, who had included such a policy among his campaign promises, upon election, found support for the change among citizen groups and in the city council; but he ran into determined opposition, too, especially from the police rank and file. Imposition of the new policy, which the new mayor accomplished, prompted the police officers' association to enlist the support of various past and present political figures, business interests, and citizens for an initiative to be put on the ballot for an upcoming election. When the initiative succeeded, it effectively nullified the new shooting policy, thereby essentially restoring the status quo ante.

A major source of intraorganizational contention in the police case has been institutional change, with the police chief as its agent and the rank and file its ostensible adversary. This has heavily implicated police unions because, in practice, the essential conflict is a struggle for effective authority between the chief and the rank and file.[3] This may not be true in every instance of internal police conflict, of course, but after the chiefs, unions generally have been the most vocal players in police power struggles.

We have reviewed various of the constraining influences on a police chief's attitudes and actions, and, by inference, on the character of policing itself. We continue this theme in the next chapter, focusing specifically on the police rank and file and police unions.

NOTES

1. The quasi-military nature of the police, in the United States at any rate, probably has less to do with organization than with social status. The police constitute a quasi-military warrior class. In common with warriors generally, they exhibit "bonds of solidarity [that] are fierce and strong. Indeed, human propensities find fullest expression in having an enemy to hate, fear, and destroy and fellow-fighters with whom to share the risks and triumphs of violent action" (McNeill, 1982, p. viii). The "enemy" of the police, of course, is the socially deviant citizen (see Bouza [1990] on the police and the "underclass"); and the status difference between police and citizenry induces a mutual alienation, which is reinforced by exclusionary guildlike patterns of association among police practitioners imbued with pride of craft and preoccupied with the "esthetics" rather than the outcomes of their occupations.

2. The tradition of political control of the police is an enduring one. "The transition [in the late nineteenth century] from the prevailing perspective of the police as an adjunct of the [local political] machine to a model of a disinterested, non-partisan and efficient agency of municipal government" was an ideological accomplishment that brought American policing under a professional model (Berman, 1987, p. 121). Monkkonen (1981) ranks so-called

progressive reform, by changing control relations, bureaucratizing, and rationalizing the operations of the uniformed police as one of two great transformations of American policing. (The first was roughly a half-century earlier, when the urban police were homogenized, put into uniforms, and integrated under centralized command structures, and began divesting themselves of welfare functions in order to concentrate on law enforcement.) Monkkonen (1981) points out, therefore, that putting the police into uniform in the mid-nineteenth century signaled *both* their authority and a bureaucratic basis for it.

3. A useful review of this struggle can be found in Part 6 of Geller's (1985) anthology on police leadership. The papers there by Bouza, a well-known "progressive" police chief, and by Kliesmet, who is President of the IUPA, AFL-CIO, deal with historical matters in informative ways that reveal sharply contrasting perspectives and interpretations that make it easy to see why one favors less and the other more power for unions in running police agencies, as well as just how wide the breach is between the two parties.

9

Chiefs and the Rank and File

Centralizing police administration around the contractual and quasi-contractual commitments endemic in complex organizations abets diffusion of rationalist managerial norms. Surely unintendedly, these have encouraged the partitioning of police work into antagonistic camps of managers and workers. Indeed, Reuss-Ianni (1983) has spoken of the emergence of "two cultures of policing: street cops and management cops." In the New York Police Department (NYPD), which she studied, street cops were concentrated at precinct levels and management cops at headquarters (see also Manning & Hawkins, 1989; we talk further about Reuss-Ianni's work in a subsequent chapter).

Coupled with these developments, police unions have become an increasingly prominent feature of the modern police agency and its environment of interested parties (Geller, 1985; Juris & Feuille, 1973; Moore & Kelling, 1983; Salerno, 1981; Walker, 1983). They have substantially increased the ability of the rank and file to coalesce and, arguably, to impose a special perspective surely on the enactment and perhaps on the conceptualization of the police role itself. This development has stimulated no little rhetoric on the revolution in blue; and more than a decade ago, Rumbaut and Bittner (1979) identified the efforts of police organizations (unions) to resist community control as a primary impediment to putting policing on a "fully reasoned basis."

EFFECTS OF POLICE UNIONS

Unions began to emerge as a significant force in the police world during the 1950s. In 1958, New York City's mayor endorsed police collective bargaining, and in 1964, he recognized the NYPD union. Police union history is longer than this, of course. Calls for unionization were heard before the turn of the century, and naturally the idea was earnestly opposed by elected officials and police administrators. The first police strike apparently occurred in 1889 in Ithaca, New York, and the much more famous Boston strike in 1919. Steady lobbying and job actions by rank-and-file police wore down the opposition and Fraternal Orders of Police (FOP) gradually transformed themselves into labor unions. By the end of the 1960s, police employee organizations were to be found in all parts of the United States; and by the end of the 1980s, more than 70% of police officers were covered by some form of collective bargaining agreement (see Levine, 1988; More, 1992).

Jermier, Cohen, Powers, and Gaines (1988) have reported that, in a "right to work environment," where union membership is not mandatory, more men than women, more married persons than single ones, and more detectives than other officers joined unions; but, in the end and overall, more than half the eligible officers did so. The single most important pre-dictor of union membership was an officer's length of service in the organi-zation—the longer the more likely; but trust (or mistrust) in the depart-ment's administration was also a factor.

Studies have shown collective bargaining to have had a variety of important impacts in police organizations, for instance on salaries, which are generally higher in unionized departments. This relationship is not a simple one, however. Feuille, Hendricks, and Delaney (1983), for instance, report that, whereas collective bargaining and arbitration do have positive effects on police salaries, market factors such as regional location, city size, and city wealth all are more important than labor relations factors in determining relative salaries. Similarly, Pugh (1980) found higher salaries in unionized departments but pointed out that unionization is most likely in heavily populated areas where both demand for services and ability to pay are high; and Ichniowski, Freeman, and Lauer (1989) concluded that bargaining laws are significant determinants of both union and nonunion employee compensation because strong bargaining legislation affects both union and nonunion department pay, the latter mainly because of threat effects. Thus substantial indirect and direct effects from police unions and collective bargaining laws can be demonstrated.

Contracts and collective bargaining inevitably put sturdy constraints on the discretion of chiefs and other administrative agents—more in some cases than in others, to be sure. However, in a study of interest arbitration in Ohio, Graham (1988) found that rulings there mostly favored the union parties (by a modest margin for police and overwhelmingly for firefighters). After a national survey of various features of 98 police collective bargaining agreements in U.S. cities with populations of 100,000 or more, Rynecki, Cairns, and Cairns (1978) described a number of ways in which these con-tracts limited the police administrator's ability to make unilateral deci-sions about police agency operation: to set standards for services offered to the public; to hire, examine, classify, promote, train, transfer, assign, and schedule personnel; to suspend, demote, discharge, or take other discipli- nary action against employees; to establish, modify, combine, or abolish job positions and classifications; to change or eliminate existing methods of operation, equipment, or facilities; or to create, modify, or delete depart- mental rules and regulations, to name some significant examples. (A later [1981] version of this report by Rynecki and Morse is available from the Police Executive Research Forum.)

Of five types of management-rights clauses Rynecki et al. were able to distinguish in the documents they reviewed, the least restrictive (on manage- ment's authority) were those that, in addition to specifying certain rights deemed important to the unilateral power of police administrators (which are virtually any of the aforementioned ones), also preserved so-called residual rights of management (i.e., any and all other rights not specified in the collective bargaining agreement). Strong management-rights con- tracts also included provisions limiting the scope of grievance arbitration. The weakest versions, while allowing management to determine certain matters, at the same time subjected those matters to grievance procedures and gave the grievance arbitration machinery broad latitude to consider decisions outside the collective bargaining agreement.

Ironically, unions generally are a strong force for contractualism and formalization in organizations, and obviously, they have contributed to the bureaucratization of police agencies (Bell, 1981). Their collective bar- gaining efforts have tended to give priority to economic issues and job security and, DeCottis and Kochan (1978) believe, have tended to treat management efforts toward professionalism as threats to job security and union prerogatives. At the same time, Jacobs (1985) points out that police unions and their hierarchy naturally work to undermine the paramilitary command chain on which police organizations customarily have been based, thereby enhancing the discretionary latitude of rank-and-file police officers.

This suggests a deeply ambiguous role for unions in the institutional theater of policing we have under review. At the same time that police unions express a conservative (or conservational) reaction to the rationalist modern- ization of police work and constraints on discretion, they serve as an (unwitting) agent of change. By contractually differentiating and formal- izing relationships within the police agency, they transform the traditional organic structure of policing and arguably the nature of police roles.

Harvie and Lawson (1978) have pointed out, though, that union inroads into management territory are not necessarily always antagonistic to general police objectives held by both chiefs and the rank and file. Also, in a study we discuss in more detail later, Halpern (1974) found cases of cooperation among unions and police executives, as well as cases of conflict. In fact, Harvie and Lawson argued that police union activity has tended to increase the autonomy of police organizations, mainly at the expense of public accountability in such areas as budgets, staffing, entrance requirements, weaponry, and discipline.

Both chiefs and unions are afloat in the same broad stream of modernization. They may fight about who is steering the boat and where it is going, but the fact is that the police labor movement has itself been chronically splintered and factionalized. There are a number of competing conferences and assemblies of police associations but no strong national union. Fallon (1984) attributes the inability of the police labor movement to coalesce to a variety of personal and philosophical disagreements among its principals but most importantly to an ingrained reluctance by cops to think of themselves as part of a national labor movement. In 1978, the International Conference of Police Associations (ICPA) split in two over affiliation with the AFL-CIO, leaving the National Association of Police Officers (NAPO) and, affiliated with the AFL-CIO, the International Union of Police Associations (IUPA). Nor has there been any national issue that could serve as a focal point around which to rally. Cory (1983) likewise noted the disagreements and conflicts that have swirled around the idea of a single national police union and concluded that statewide organizations may be more important.

All politics is local after all. Institutional change is general, diffuse, and implicit. In the decentralized context of American policing, it is concrete local conditions of employment and local personalities that are most apt to be the drivers of police unionization and action. Still, if not now evident, a national issue capable of broadly galvanizing coalescence could yet emerge around cops' basic and common interest in the fundamental role of the police in American society and an increasing involvement of police officers and their organizations in conservative law-and-order politics at national as well as local levels (Harvie & Lawson, 1978).

UNIONS AND POLICE ROLES

Among the many studies of police unionism, four, all done in the 1970s, stand out as especially interesting for our purposes. Each of them addresses the key question of how the role of the police in society is decided. The first study is an empirical one by Juris and Feuille (1973), which was designed "to chronicle and interpret . . . activities and impacts of police unions in twenty-two cities." In addition to characterizing the then-general state of labor relations in police agencies, this descriptive work focused attention on the relative power of actors in the police network, especially chiefs and the rank and file. Of particular interest to Juris and Feuille were union impacts on the chief's ability to manage and on the formulation of law-enforcement policy.

Like other, more general studies of public sector unions, Juris and Feuille found that unions have manifestly and significantly narrowed management discretion. However, as to policy, they suggested that union impacts had been mainly indirect. By creating an environment of tension in the police-community network, Juris and Feuille concluded that police unions inhibit and control policy initiatives by other actors, including both police management and elected officials. An illustration of this can be seen in the experience with Proposition 13 in California. Swimmer (1983) learned from his research on it that the political and economic power of unions will partially determine where cuts are made in a financial squeeze simply because municipal authorities "will determine cuts on a politically expedient basis." As a common result (or so it would seem from our observations of police decision making), local officials tend to avoid police policy engagements. Such issues, Juris and Feuille point out,

> are part of larger political questions: Not civilian review but whether the police or civilians will make law enforcement policy; not weapons policy but the question of who determines the conditions under which fatal force will be allowed. The resolution of these issues will not be a function of collective bargaining unless the parties, especially management, make a conscious effort to bring these subjects into the bargaining process. In the absence of such conscious effort, they will remain political issues to be fought out in the political arena. (Juris & Feuille, 1973, p. 12)

Thus Juris and Feuille highlight what may be called the issue of police in society. Their research, however, oriented as it was to descriptions of police labor systems, resource allocation, and terms-and-conditions collective bargaining, did not address the issue of police roles, except in very broad terms.

Another study that did address the social role of police and their unions, albeit more conceptually than empirically, was Levi's (1977). She used case studies and historical reviews to analyze what she called "bureaucratic insurgency" (unionization) in the public sector generally and in police agencies in particular. She traced insurgency to a customary array of relative-power instigators to unionism, plus, in the police case especially, its utility as a stress-controlling tactic. All this she related to forms of political action, asking (but, it must be said, not really answering) why such action varied in strength in different times and places.

Levi called police unions the most interesting example of bureaucratic insurgency because they seem so unlikely (as well as being among the last public employee groups to unionize). Unlikely or not, she judged that police unions were becoming increasingly powerful and militant (the two traits being intercorrelated, she thought), and in quest of broader *political* power. She foresaw police unions, therefore, confronting not only particularistic terms and conditions of immediate employment (e.g., in collective bargaining), but also, and more importantly, the public definition of their social role. In the police-community network, she perceived police actors to have become both wider-ranging and more public-oriented, as police union sponsorship of electoral initiatives, endorsements of candidates, and other political actions imply.

Somewhat in the spirit of Levi's study, but focused on the two basic issues central to Juris and Feuille's research—that is, limitation of police management discretion and control of policy—was Halpern's (1974) doctoral dissertation. His in-depth case studies of police association and department leaders in three big-city police agencies revealed tendencies toward conflict (e.g., with regard to *internal* performance review), but also tendencies toward collaboration (e.g., with regard to *external* civilian reviews). Halpern's findings led him to caution against overemphasizing the adversarial nature of relations between police management and employee organizations. He himself directed attention instead to the operation among them of mutual co-optive strategies. Halpern's argument was simply to the effect that patterns of relations between police administrators and employee organizations (including unions) will be variable, depending on the issue and the distribution of interests regarding it.

In another Ph.D. dissertation, Reiner (1978), as a student of Michael Banton in England, studied the Police Federation of the United Kingdom. His was essentially an individual-level analysis of the beliefs, attitudes, and other sentiments of federation members. He sought to find a "motive to unionization" in the contradictory position of police in the United Kingdom class structure, where (not unlike in the United States, actually) they are responsible on the one hand for conservation of the social system but are also workers (alienated laborers?) subject to "discipline and control in which they have little to say." Reiner, therefore, set out to analyze the police officer "from the perspective of his situation as an employee, which generates pressures that can conflict with the demands of his role as a law enforcer" (p. 4).

What he found was that the "extent to which policemen feel they need and wish to have trade union representation to protect and advance their interests" (p. 9) is variable and has complicated linkages with other factors. Nonetheless, however that may be, and despite barriers to unionism, which

Reiner discusses, more than two thirds of his respondents believed unions should have an *institutionalized* say in running their departments. This and other of his findings prompted him to forecast among police rank and file a growing militancy and demands for "assertion of a police voice on social policy." (A recent case study by Thompson [1988] suggests rather similarly that police union militancy in the United States arises in an environment of dissatisfaction, combined with beliefs that collective bargaining is a matter more of cynical political gamesmanship than of rational adjudication.)

Each of these studies suggested tendencies toward increasingly militant unionist orientations by police officers. Each provides indications of combinations by rank-and-file officers to limit both the command discretion of police leaders and their autonomy in policymaking, especially as regards prescription of the police officer's role. Collectively, they also suggested increasingly direct public policy involvement by police associations; and Halpern's study at least implied that the relations among actors within the police agency and between those actors and others in the policy community network may be complex—adversarial or cooperative, depending on the circumstances.

EFFECTS OF UNIONS ON THE POLICE ROLE IN SOCIETY

Although suggestive, none of these studies (or others) actually explored the network of police-community relations within which public policy and police roles are shaped. Consequently, the question of how much real effect, if any, police unions have on the fundamental conceptualization of the role of the police in society was not addressed. Presumption on the point, of course, is generally to the effect that union influence has been substantial:

> As late as the mid-1960s police chiefs had virtually unlimited power to run their departments. . . . Today police chiefs are severely constrained. Not only are many important issues subject to collective bargaining, but police unions exert enormous informal influence both within the department and the community at large. Police unions are here to stay; we cannot ignore [them]. (William O. Douglas Institute for the Study of Contemporary Social Problems, 1984, p. 27)

Despite this assessment, however, there is surprisingly little information about how police unions (or anything else) affect the police role in society (if they have), or about the role outcomes experienced by police officers.

10

Shaping Police Roles

Chief Anthony Bouza (1985) quotes one of his colleagues as saying that "the only inherent rights of management are those labor does not bargain away from them." He goes on to conclude from his own review of police union activities in the United States, and the "ebbs and flows" of union strength and aggressiveness, that there has been "a rising tide of militance beginning in the late 1960s" (p. 278). He suggests that "at this moment in history unions are ascendant and the chiefs are playing catch-up" (p. 279). Acknowledging the legitimacy of police unions and their interests, Bouza nevertheless expresses concern about "the willingness of labor to make inappropriate incursions into management enclaves" and asserts that "it is not too much to say that the unions have made the full scope of police operations their realm" (p. 278).

Bouza sees the issues here as a matter of role definitions, and so does Robert Kleismet, the president of the IUPA (AFL-CIO). In his rebuttal to Bouza in the Geller book (1985) he divides the argument about union impacts into four areas: their affects on salaries and conditions of employment, on administration of the police agency, on policies, and on service delivery. The bottom line, Kleismet contends, is whether and how unions and collective bargaining have affected the last of these. He adds, however, that answering this question is tough because of disagreements about what those services—about what the role of the police—should be.

POLICE ROLES

Roles are learned attributes that are "characteristic of persons in a context" (Biddle, 1979). They vary and are analyzable on three dimensions: (a) *descriptive,* or what someone does; (b) *prescriptive,* or what someone should do; and (c) *cathectic,* or what someone likes to do. Hence, useful distinctions may be drawn regarding the dispositional or functional aspects of roles, the ways they are performed, and how people feel about them.

The content of the police role is neither fixed nor universal. It necessarily varies with local conditions and preferences and, to an extent, with the discretion of individual officers. Its elastic quality is caught by Bayley's characterization of the police as "a group authorized in the name of a territorial community to utilize force . . . *to handle whatever needs doing*" (Bayley, 1979, p. 113; emphasis added).

Wilson (1968), as we have seen, suggests three kinds of things that need doing and that may therefore constitute basic descriptive, cathectic, or prescriptive components of contemporary police roles: law enforcement, order maintenance, and service delivery. Others make similar proposals (Banton, 1964; Bittner, 1970, 1990).

Wilson (1968) proposes a typology of policing styles, using the law enforcement, order maintenance, service delivery distinctions. He suggests that police agencies tend to adopt one of three styles by emphasizing one of the role components more than the others. There is a "legalistic" style of policing, which emphasizes enforcing the law; a "watchman" style, which emphasizes maintaining order; and a "service" style, which emphasizes giving help. Hence the role of the police in a community may vary substantially from locality to locality, depending on their stylistic emphases (Brown, 1981). Within any particular police department, individuals and groups, chiefs and rank and file may also have varying preferences for these different styles—and they may and do fight about them.

The police collectively are at once instruments of public policy—public authorities—and partisans interested in shaping that policy and its normative premises in their interests. They are, of course, also interpreters of policy applications and, hence, its operational definers. When one police department found itself faced with embarrassing disclosures about its intelligence files, for instance, and came under pressure from the mayor to control them, it sought to defuse public displeasure and agitation toward prohibiting the department from collecting intelligence information. The department mounted a public display of active *internal* policy development, sending selected officers to national organizations (e.g., the IACP) for courses in file structure and management, conferring informally with members of other experienced police agencies, retaining a special consultant on specifications for intelligence operations for political activities, reviewing matters with the city attorney as to liability questions, consulting with the state criminal justice agency, and placing a member on a city task force on systems that included representatives of the public—all the while continuing to develop the files.

VARIATION IN THE POLICE ROLE

Variation in the content of police roles carries important implications for police-community relations, internal police operations, police morale, and the quality and quantity of law enforcement (Black, 1980). Moore and Kelling (1983), as we have noted, argue, for instance, that a police strategy of emphasizing law enforcement neither serves to deter crime nor is suc- cessful in apprehending offenders. It does, however, they maintain, result in the neglect of many constabulary tasks once traditional to police work. It also may have the unintended consequence of weakening the bonds between police and private citizens.

In any event, a focus on fighting crime may lead to policies (e.g., authorized equipment, use of force, arrest) designed to enhance police ability to apprehend suspects, but which also create community tension (Wilson, 1968, 1983). Ironically, too, it has been argued, an emphasis on law enforcement may reduce the effectiveness of the police in solving crimes. Stressing this role, Wilson and Kelling (1982) contend, may weaken bonds between the police and the community to the point where necessary assistance from victims and witnesses is withheld. (This argument, as we show later, is at the base of controversial proposals to redefine the police role as a community-oriented service delivery and problem-solving function.)

HOW ROLES ARE SHAPED

Obviously, some heavy thinking and argument have gone on about the subject of police roles, and many aspects of the police role have been studied. Unhappily, the results of these studies tell us little about relationships between factors such as unionization and specific variations in the police role or between variations in the police role and the outcomes individuals experience by performing it (Wycoff, 1982).

Generally speaking, ideas about roles are communicated among the individual and institutional members of social networks—that is, their rosters of actors. The interacting members of these networks (or role sets) normally differ in their power relative to one another. The result is an ongoing asymmetrical influence and bargaining process over individual and institutional social functions. Some writers refer to this interchange as "role sending" (Katz & Kahn, 1978). We prefer to call it "role making" (see also Pfeffer & Salancik, 1978; Weick, 1979). It is this process of role making, and who influences it how, that is basic to Bouza's and Kleismet's debate.

TESTING THE EFFECTS OF
UNIONIZATION ON POLICE ROLES

With particular reference to the police role, our own research (Hunt & Magenau, 1983a, 1983b; Hunt, McCadden, & Mordaunt, 1983; Magenau & Hunt, 1989) has suggested a preference among rank-and-file police officers for a law-enforcement role. Also, our case studies provide examples of how the rank and file have influenced specific decisions in the direction of greater emphasis on this role. Assuming, too, that unionization has increased the power of the rank and file relative to other network actors, it effectively enhances their ability to shape the police role in ways they desire.

Taking these ideas as a point of departure, we can state a series of propositions about the seemingly likely effects of unionization on the police role in society.

1. Unionization can be expected to increase the ability of the rank and file to influence the content of the police role specifically toward greater emphasis on law enforcement and less emphasis on order maintenance and service delivery. That is, for reasons of cognitive consistency, the rank and file can be expected to believe that the important goals of policing are the same as the ones they personally prefer.

2. As a consequence of this tendency toward consistency, unionization should also result in increased importance being placed on law enforcement and decreased importance being placed on order maintenance and service delivery as goals of policing.

3. Regardless of their specific preferences, however, union power should allow police officers to achieve greater correspondence between the descriptive dimension of their roles (what they do) and the prescriptive and cathectic dimensions (what they feel they need and like to do).

4. We may also expect police unions to try to protect the professional autonomy of their members by preserving the discretion of police officers in determining how they do their jobs and by keeping job descriptions vaguely defined. In concert with greater autonomy and role clarity, police officers in unionized settings may, therefore, be expected to experience fewer external influences (e.g., from higher authorities, courts, rules) and more internal (personal) influences (e.g., intuition, experience) on the way they do their work.

5. To the extent that unions are effective in influencing the police role in the ways suggested, then arguably the rank and file should experience greater satisfaction with supervisory and personnel practices, should have stronger feelings of recognition and accomplishment, should report more job satisfaction, and should also have higher levels of work motivation.

6. However, because the preferences of other network actors may be contrary to the rank and file, they may feel less satisfaction with police-community relations.

A SURVEY OF POLICE DEPARTMENTS

In order to evaluate these six propositions about the effects of unions on police roles, we defined a subpopulation of American police departments from which a suitable sample of respondents could be selected. We sought to control contextual variables that might be related to the police role by selecting from the 171 U.S. cities having 100,000 or more population (according to the 1980 census), a group of departments with similar community environments, as indexed by 26 variables derived from 1980 census data, crime statistics from the 1982 *FBI Uniform Crime Reports,* and a measure of each city's financial condition, taken from the 1982 edition of *Moody's General Obligation Bond Rating.* (A detailed description of this research may be found in Magenau & Hunt, 1992.)

Using this information, statistical methods were used to identify 15 clusters of cities having similar characteristics. One particular group of 22 cities seemed peculiarly appropriate for study because of its manageable size and good mix of union and nonunion departments, as identified by Rynecki and Morse (1981). The chief of police in each of these 22 cities was contacted, and 15 agreed to participate in the study. Most of them provided rosters of rank-and-file police officers so that random samples of up to 250 officers could be drawn from each department. (In departments having fewer than 250 officers, we sampled 100% of the rank and file.)

Questionnaires using some standard and some specially designed items covering a wide range of personal and role-related matters, work conditions and activities, and work/role outcomes (satisfaction, influence, police-community relations, and so forth) were distributed by a departmental contact person during work hours to specifically named individuals in each department, who then mailed their completed questionnaires directly to us.

The percentage of usable questionnaires returned from the 15 departments ranged from 17.4 to 65.0. Interestingly, department-specific completion rates were unrelated to any role outcome measures (e.g., job satisfaction), but they were higher from those departments whose officers regarded the law enforcement aspect of their work as more important than they were from those where order maintenance or service delivery were preferred. Questionnaire completion rates were also higher in departments where rank-and-file memberships in work-related organizations was high, and where external agencies or factors were widely perceived to be influential on how the work of the departments was done. (Statistical analyses controlled for the effects of these differential completion rates, so the relationships reported between other variables should not be biased by variation in these rates.)

Findings of the Survey

On the whole, the substantive results of the survey gave little support to the idea that police unions literally shape the police role. What formal representation by a union does seem to do, however, is to lessen police officers' apparent need for personal involvement in work-related organizations, including unions.

Unions also seem to have positive effects on police officers' role outcomes. Not surprisingly, perhaps, these include reports of more satisfactory supervisory and personnel practices and greater job satisfaction, but, more remarkably, they also include better community relations and higher work motivation. Hence, unions may not only improve the working environment for their members but also may actually provide a context for better managerial practice that can improve motivation and the relationship of the police with the local community.

Moreover, we found no evidence that involvement in work-related organizations, including unions, was motivated by dissatisfaction with work. In fact, the opposite seems to be true. Those officers who were more involved and active tended to be individuals who also experienced more positive role outcomes in their work. Involvement in a union and other work-related organizations seems to be motivated by attraction to and identification with policing rather than by unhappiness with work, as many commentators would have it. On the other hand, though, we also found that officers' involvement in police work-related organizations is associated with less positive perceptions of police-community relations.

Minority and female officers did not differ much from other officers in the ways they perceived their roles, but they did seem to experience less satisfaction from playing them. Assignment to patrol duty also seems to contribute to poorer role outcomes in the shape, for instance, of less discretion and greater order-maintenance responsibilities. The negative role experiences of those assigned to patrol duty represent a significant challenge for police administrators because more than 60% of those responding to our survey held such assignments.

Regarding tenure as a police officer, the survey findings were both complex and intriguing. Longer-tenure officers reported *less* actual involvement in all three types of police role content, tending, evidently, to hold desk jobs that have fewer operational responsibilities. At the same time, however, they report *more* congruence with respect to the law-enforcement aspect of their jobs; and, while they are less involved in police roles, they belong to more work-related organizations than do less senior officers, and they are more active in them (and might, therefore, be assumed to have more friendships). Yet, despite these apparent advantages, more senior officers generally experienced more negative role outcomes than did their junior counterparts, a finding suggestive of burnout with longer service in police work. Who then is the unhappiest police officer? Well, according to our data, she is a minority group member with long organizational tenure assigned to patrol duty. That these particular personal characteristics are the ones that point most directly to dissatisfaction implies significant challenges for the human resource managers of police departments.

In another finding, criminal activity and community disturbances are generally more prevalent in the evening and early morning hours. Later shift assignments can, therefore, be expected to entail greater involvement in hard-core police work; and our data showed this: more involvement in law enforcement and order maintenance, less in service delivery. The data also showed that the higher the proportion of a department's members who were involved in later shift assignments, the poorer were the department's estimates of its community relations; and these same departments tended also to be ones in which the members indicated that their involvement in work-related organizations was increasing.

There were suggestions that less positive community relations may be explained by officers' greater involvement in the order-maintenance that later shift assignments entail. The data indicated, too, that there is a relationship between perceptions of poor-quality community relations and police officers tending to increase their involvement in work-related organizations, as if the perception of a hostile community environment somehow motivates the increasing involvement.

Between larger and smaller departments, there are a few things about role dimensions that are worth mentioning. For one thing, larger departments placed more emphasis on service delivery than did smaller ones, and their members seemed less interested in work-related organizations. Also, there was greater congruence (consistency between preferences and practices) for the law-enforcement role in larger departments. Because there were no significant differences between larger and smaller departments in actual law-enforcement activity, evidently larger departments simply are better able to provide a match between actual involvement in law enforcement and at levels of it that are desired or considered appropriate by their officers. Role outcome data, in fact, did suggest that larger departments provide a more satisfying work environment.

Police Role Preferences

Our data provide at least limited support for the assumption, which in fact is a common one, that police officers prefer the law-enforcement role over the order-maintenance and service-delivery roles: Law enforcement is the *only* dimension of role content we found not *negatively* related to role outcomes, and the *only* content that *motivates* police officers. The other two role content dimensions were related only to *negative* outcomes. Dissatisfaction was most widespread for order-maintenance activities, which, according to our results, appear to be the least desired of the three types of role content. This obviously implies that it may be difficult to interest rank-and-file police officers in police reforms such as Wilson and Kelling's (1982), which emphasize order maintenance and peacekeeping. At the same time, however, other data suggest (unsurprisingly) that order maintenance can be motivating *if* there is congruence for the role—that is, if people want to do it.

As for the general importance of law-enforcement, order-maintenance, and service-delivery goals of policing, as we have said, our findings suggest that police officers vote for law enforcement. Nevertheless, the three goals relate somewhat differently to individual role outcomes. Individuals who attach more importance to law enforcement report higher job satisfaction and motivation; those who place greater emphasis on order maintenance/ service delivery perceive better quality police-community relations, and have more positive views of supervisory and personnel practices. Thus belief in the importance of law enforcement seems to be associated with outcomes that are more satisfying to the *individual* officer, while an emphasis on order maintenance/service delivery seems to contribute to better *inter-personal* relationships.

Believing in the importance of both law enforcement and order maintenance/service delivery, however, relates to a greater sense of recognition and accomplishment. Also, despite the differences in their relationship to other role outcomes, police officers who believe in the importance of the goals of their work, whether those goals are law enforcement, order maintenance, or service delivery, generally experience more positive role outcomes. Nor do our data suggest that an emphasis on law enforcement (or any other particular goal for that matter) is deleterious to the quality of police-community relationships. Regarding whether order-maintenance and service-delivery orientations contribute to better police-community relationships, however, the data are inconsistent. It appears to be the case that those whose *job* it is to maintain order are *less* positive about community relations, while those who *believe* that order maintenance/service delivery are important goals, whether they do it or not, have *more* positive views of community relations.

On the subject of police-officer discretion in how they do their work, police officers do in fact seem to experience more positive role outcomes when they feel they have more discretion. Furthermore, we find indications that they will use that greater discretion in ways that are beneficial to community relations rather than harmful to them. Not only that, a preference for autonomy does not imply any lack of clarity about job responsibilities or being left to an individual's intuition and common sense in carrying out police work. Police officers, in fact, report more positive role outcomes when their job responsibilities are clear and external influences work to provide guidance. What is more, clear expectations and the presence of external influences on police behavior are associated with more positive community relations.

A FEW CONCLUSIONS ON
POLICE ROLES AND UNIONS

What we have seen here is that variations in the police role affect the morale of rank-and-file police officers and the way they perceive police-community relations. As we expected, law enforcement is the preferred role for most rank-and-file police officers, and it appears to be what motivates them in their work. Actual involvement in other roles seems, on the whole, a negative police experience that may make widespread conversion to problem- or community-oriented strategies of policing difficult to accomplish.

Importantly, however, an emphasis on law enforcement does not necessarily cause deterioration of police-community relations. Also, while it is true that a police officer's involvement in order maintenance may be associated with negative views of police-community relations, there is, at the same time, evidence that a department's placing greater importance on order maintenance and service delivery can be associated with more positive views of police-community relations. The key seems to be whether the officer's involvement is a product of explicit departmental policy.

Thus from this research at any rate, we see little indication of the dramatic impacts of police unions described by the William O. Douglas Institute for the Study of Contemporary Social Problems (1984) or the viewings with alarm of many police chiefs, public administrators, and commentators. In fact, unionization, per se, does not seems to have very much at all to do with variation in the police role. Unionization is, however, associated with positive role outcomes among police officers, *including* a perception of better police-community relations.

So if unionization, per se, is a red herring, what is going on to make police labor-management relations so tense? Nothing else, of course, than institutional changes around but manifest in police agencies. Unions (and other employee associations) focus and give voice to the rank and file's concerns about control of their circumstances—not only the usual terms and conditions of their work, but its essential nature. Unions and their activities express but they do not cause the fundamental social conflicts that broadly define the relations between police administrators and rank-and-file officers. If police unions disappeared, the basic conflicts about what policing is and how to do it would remain. The arguments would simply find other structures and means of expression in the contemporary culture of policing in America.

11

The American Culture of Policing
Content and Conflict

Culture **is to societies** more or less what *personality* is to individual people: a kind of collective quality, distinctive on the whole, but neither altogether homogeneous nor unique in its elements. Not an easy or rigorous scientific concept, the idea of *culture* nevertheless serves to acknowledge the broad thematic similarities and contrasts among social systems and their members that seem so evident in common experience.

In its early anthropological usage, *culture* referred mainly to the manners, morals, and customs of whole societies. Today the term is used more freely. Especially since the 1970s, it has become common to speak even of individual organizations as having distinct cultures: "hidden yet unifying theme[s] that provide meaning, direction, and mobilization" (Kilmann et al., 1985, p. ix) to guide their performance. In his book *Bureaucracy* (1989), James Q. Wilson, for example, asserts that every organization has one or more cultures that result from the predispositions of their members, their technologies, and their situational imperatives.

In the case of American police departments, we earlier noted Reuss-Ianni's (1983) proposal that at least two primary cultures exist: one a street-cop culture, concentrated in the precincts, and the other a management cop culture, concentrated at headquarters. We return shortly to the specifics of Reuss-Ianni's idea, but first we need to consider whether and in what way it makes sense, on the one hand, to generalize the way she does about police culture, or, conversely, to regard individual police departments as culturally distinct.

IS THERE AN AMERICAN CULTURE OF POLICING?

With thousands of individual police departments in a big diverse country, the police in America are necessarily heterogeneous. Their organizations vary greatly in size from work forces counted in single digits to others in five figures. Their complexity as organizations varies, and so do the rules according to which they operate. The training of their officers and their codes of practice differ. Some departments affiliate with the Police Executive Research Forum (PERF), while others would not dream of doing so. Hence, the police in America are inevitably diverse culturally. How diverse are they? Is each police agency sui generis?

Not really. Factors external to individual police agencies work to impel and consolidate the manifest characteristics and collective status of the police as a social institution. These same factors encourage not unanimity, but a broadly coherent complex of beliefs, customs, norms, and outlooks among police officers, certainly in major U.S. cities, along with mechanisms for the reinforcement and diffusion of these attitudes and sentiments (toward rookies, for instance). The result can reasonably be called a "culture" of policing in America: a broadly "distinctive way of seeing and responding to the world" (Wilson, 1989, p. 90) that is widely distributed among police officers in the United States, regardless of their particular local conditions.

CULTURAL DIFFERENTIATION

Cultures are only rarely uniform, however. Discontinuities of conditions and practices from one time or place to another ensure that even within themselves they will encompass variants of one or another kind: regional and local variations, subcultures, countercultures, and whatnot. Indeed, any differentiated element of a larger social system—a department in a factory, a professional group—must by definition describe a variant of its larger culture.

In fact, it is in this somewhat hierarchic sense that so-called organizational or corporate or occupational cultures are plausible concepts. As social institutions, corporations, municipal governments, and police departments are culture producers as well as culture carriers, and they may, therefore, describe more or less easily distinguishable variant cultures. Indeed, the corporate culture literature sometimes speaks of strong and weak forms of culture, presumably implying something about the visibility of their norms, beliefs, and values, as well perhaps as the pertinence of their specifically local culture to the organization's performance.

So just as cultures, organizational or other, should not be conceived as monolithic, neither should they be regarded in isolation from their contexts. For, although they may be culture producers, organizations are first and foremost culture *carriers*. Patterns within a particular organization are mainly continuous with some larger cultural context and are, in fact, part of the same cultural fabric. Happenings within an organization simply are not peculiar to it, are not independent of the cultural frame that surrounds it. There is coherence to this cultural frame, but the pieces of it are not necessarily causes of one another.

More precisely to the present subject, an *occupational* culture of policing based in commonly accepted definitions of its nature, purposes, and conditions can be said to overarch particular organizational variations and to promote similarities among police everywhere in America (although it may differ in important ways from counterparts in other nations). Expressions of this occupational culture in different American police agencies will necessarily show coloration by local organizational, political, and other contextual influences. Like cultures generally, the culture of policing is differentiated into variants or subcultures, based on rank (command vs. rank and file), function (patrol vs. administration), and various factors associated with local environments and organizational auspices (e.g., elected vs. appointed chiefs). These subcultural variants each will be distinctive in some ways, yet at the same time they all are more generally alike: variations on a theme.

THE CRAFT BASIS OF
TRADITIONAL POLICE CULTURE

Discussions of culture in organizational and managerial contexts too often are simplistic to the point of trivializing the idea. One hears a great deal about corporate heroes or TQM projects changing organizational cultures, as if that were quite an easy thing to do. In fact, cultures are highly resilient. Broader social forces over which local organizations have little real control severely constrain their choices and actions.

Indeed, the well-known father of Theory Z, William Ouchi (1979), has been inclined to argue that cultures in any organization-specific sense are, in fact, rare birds. Ouchi perceives three distinct organizational forms (we call them "cultures") that correspond to three basic ways that organizations govern exchanges between and among parties. One is a system that is externally controlled by market mechanisms; a second is also externally controlled, but by bureaucratic means (rules and contracts). The third organizational form or culture, which Ouchi calls a "clan," is a small, stable, long-standing, unified grouping having high levels of interpersonal goal congruence. This clan relies mainly on socializing its members—an internal-control device—in order to regulate their particular transactions by building its norms and values into them. Only the clan, Ouchi thinks, can be meaningfully said to have a distinct *local* culture. The others, which make up the bulk of all corporations and other organizations, Ouchi suggests, can only be seen as culture carriers—that is, as expressions of general cultural patterns.

These ideas have an important bearing on the character and origins of a culture of policing. Recall our suggestion that police departments resemble craft organizations, that their structures and work methods express the customs and requirements of craftlike modes of production. *Craft* is an occupational and a structural concept that is more general than that of an organization. Hence, the latter will tend to express the properties of the former.

Organic craft-based organizations approximate Ouchi's clans and so are likely to be strong cultures. Wilson (1989) captures the significance of this by pointing out that "when a single culture is broadly shared and warmly endorsed it is a mission" (p. 110). He was speaking of a chief-driven organi- zational mission when he made this point, but the larger implication is that, regardless of its source, a strong culture will drive a local organization's view of its mission.

According to Wilson, "FBI agents behaved as if J. Edgar Hoover were looking over their shoulders, in part because the agents believed that was the right way to behave" (p. 110). It may have been (as Wilson suggested) that these agents were responding to the influence of an uncommonly powerful individual in special circumstance, but it may instead be that the leader was principally a craft master and exemplar of a tacit occupational ethos to which one and all were (and are) implicitly committed. Chiefs in such circumstances simply benefit from natural leadership attributions (see Meindl & Ehrlich, 1987).

In any case, the sway of a strong generalized occupational craft culture that recapitulates itself locally will heavily constrain the particulars of individual local police organizations and also the ability of market-oriented (e.g., community-oriented) or bureaucratically oriented chiefs and management cops to affect them.

ACCULTURATING THE POLICE

Cultures are acquired characteristics of individuals. They are learned by a process called "socialization" or "acculturation." Some of this acculturation is formal, but most of it is implicit. Bad apples among police officers, Bouza (1990) maintains, for instance, usually are filtered out of police departments at selection (by background checks, testing, etc.). "Those later found unfit are veterans" who, he insists, have been "shaped by the agency rather than by their genes or pre-entrance proclivities. . . . The brutes have not slipped through the agency's filter. Rather, they've been shaped by the organization's culture" (p. 69). In other words, they have been acculturated.

This acculturation is an intergenerational process by which individuals are indoctrinated with or simply acquire particular patterns of beliefs, values, attitudes, and practices. As Bouza describes it, the acculturation of police officers emphasizes that the thing to be is not "ethical" but a "stand-up guy" (p. 72). It takes place via formal training, role-modeling, and by the actions and lore of older cops. As for the part played by chiefs, Bouza rightly believes that "employees tend to respond to the value system transmitted in the daily actions of the hierarchy [more] than to written policy" (1990, p. 49). He stressed the potent role of symbols (e.g., the car driven by the chief—Bouza drove an old one; the new ones went to operational uses, by which symbolism he intended to communicate his values). He also emphasized the way in which ethical standards are reflected in and reinforced by a chief's daily actions (what and who he or she rewards), and the extent to which a chief conveys clear behavioral standards by consistency in disciplinary actions.

Both Bouza and Reuss-Ianni (1983) heavily emphasize the key role played by field-training specialists in ensuring "continuity of the informal rules" regardless of any formal police training curricula. As in any craft organization, the primary means of acquiring relevant beliefs, values, and skills is an apprenticeship. It is the combination of apprenticeship and the always present informal secondary control system of custom and on-the-job practice that continuously governs police acculturation (Kerstetter, 1985). "Rookie cops are told this the first day on patrol: 'Forget what you learned in the police academy,' veteran partners or sergeants will tell them. 'I'll show you what police work is really all about' " (Wilson, 1989, p. 37). Administrators may try to prevent this "street-corner socialization," Wilson observes, but they have little luck in doing so.

THE TRADITIONAL CRAFT
CULTURE OF AMERICAN POLICING

"Cops," according to the marvelously quotable Tony Bouza, "work in a world shrouded with mystery and power, value orthodoxy, loyalty, obedience, and silence," and permit "no winds of change" (1990, p. 1). The culture of a "typical police agency," he declared, is both "powerful and self-reinforcing" and "as hermetically sealed as the Vatican" (p. 44).

Policing, first of all, is *not* customarily a lateral-entry occupation. Virtually everyone starts at the bottom as an apprentice, including the chiefs, most of whom come up from the ranks. Of 117 police chiefs surveyed by Enter (1986a), two thirds had risen through the ranks of a single agency. Another quarter were lateral moves to chief from a supervisory position in another police department. Only a small fraction came from anything other than a local police department (e.g., a federal law-enforcement agency), and none of the chiefs came with anything other than a law-enforcement background. Chief Daryl Gates's successor in Los Angeles, Willie Williams, previously chief in Philadelphia, is the first chief of the LAPD in 40 years from outside its ranks, and Gates himself was the first in recent memory to have competition from outside. Interestingly (although perhaps not surprisingly), Enter (1986b) found that outsider chiefs had higher educational levels and had had more exposure to important staff assignments than did insiders, who, however, had longer career paths.

In any event, homogeneous and tightly knit, police departments have remained "remarkably stable, white, male institutions" (p. 34). The numbers of women has increased steadily in the past decade or so, according to Martin (1989), but the pace has been slow (still only some 8 or 9 percent), especially at supervisory levels; and career paths appear to vary by gender, with men moving along investigative tracks and women into administrative and staff roles. Blacks constitute about 13.5% of all police ranks (a growth of some 40% since the early 1980s), and Hispanics 5.5% of the total (*The New York Times,* April 25, 1991, p. B10).

The police are well equipped with special myths, symbols, and signals of membership—uniforms, badges, their own argot, stories, heroes, rituals, codes, and pigeonholes (e.g., for "assholes," which is anyone who flunks the street cop's "attitude tests"—i.e., anyone "who fails to treat the cop with the proper measure of respect, or is truculent or challenging" [Bouza, 1990, p. 3], and how to deal with them). On the whole, a staunchly parochial and insular lot, cops feel that no outsider understands them or their craft. Not surprisingly, most cops' friends are other cops. Defensive and scornful of civilians, and especially the press (which is seen as an exploitative enemy [Reuss-Ianni, 1983]), the police protect their turf and "don't take real or imagined assaults on their authority lightly" (Bouza, 1990, p. 3). Disorderly conduct statutes, Bouza suggests, "arm cops with weapons against those they've defined as 'assholes' " (p. 8).

Police officers are "welded together by dangerous experiences and shared secrets," says Bouza (p. 67). Solidarity, esprit-de-corps, camaraderie, fraternal spirit, and interpersonal bonding all are prominent feelings among those engaged in the manly pursuits of police work. Their dangerous occupation requires dependable support and unquestioning loyalty: Cops help cops, right or wrong. (Reuss-Ianni [1983] reports, for example, on the trial of a New York City police officer who was accused of killing a suspect in custody.

In the course of the trial, several cops admitted lying to a Grand Jury, explaining that it was accepted practice to commit perjury in order to protect a fellow officer.) Reinforced by a career structure that works to bond them together, and by mutual dependency for backup and safety, cops' "us versus them" worldview fosters an especially profound depth of feeling between partners (which, as Bouza observes, complicates the entry of women into the ranks).

Cops automatically expect support from their chief (who should, of course, be a "regular guy") and are unforgiving if they do not get it. They "accept the myths circulating around them because resistance carries a risk of ostracism" (Bouza, 1990, p. 72); and they "grouse about their jobs and counsel casual acquaintances against taking them, but inevitably encourage their relatives and loved ones to enter the department" (p. 68).

At the same time that police officers are profoundly sensible of a "brotherhood in blue" made up of "stand-up cops who don't turn their buddies in" (Bouza, 1990, p. 71), Bittner (1990) argues that they all are at base individual entrepreneurs—individualists who happen also to be interdependent. They understand that they are on their own and must be able to take care of themselves. Their image of themselves as a "thin blue line" between society and chaos demands of them an attitude of "unintimidated self-sufficiency." Also, as Bittner points out, cops, especially in the uniformed patrol, "work alone or in pairs, among strangers," and "the very same people who expect to know their children's teacher, their clergyman, their physician, their mail carrier, and most other people who respond to their needs, do not expect to know the police officers who work in their neighborhoods" (1990, p. 12).

Bittner describes police departments as "complicated systems of secret sharing." Gates (1992) insists that this is not and never was true, at least in the LAPD, and in any case, is misunderstood. What he sees is a system of peer discipline and judgment calls about what behavior to report and to whom, not a categorical Code of Silence. Nevertheless, Bouza persists in noting that, like a mafia, a "veil of silence surround[s] police agencies" (1990, p. 47): an intense "code of loyalty, silence, secretiveness, and isolation reigns" (p. 73) and anathematizes its violators ("snitchers"). Line cops do not talk about peers in the presence of ranking officers or any one else partly for "fear of disclosure of embarrassing facts," yet matters that never can be mentioned to outsiders are shop talk among cops themselves (e.g., the infamous mobile digital transmissions among Los Angeles patrol officers following the March 1991 Rodney King episode).

Bittner (1990) noted, however, that while there is an "infinite variety of contingently collusive arrangements that always bind the entire personnel against outsiders," they also "solidify a plethora of internal schisms and conspiracies" (p. 148). "Nobody," Bittner added, "tells anybody else

more than he absolutely has to" (p. 149), and that includes partners. Cops'
solidarity is risk-relative. Generally speaking, Bittner stressed, everyone
is on his or her own, and everyone has information that is not shared,
except perhaps as a favor, but "no one has a claim on it."

Cops, Wilson (1989) noted, quickly learn the value of being wary and
skeptical, that people lie, cheat, and betray. They also have a correlative
need to "deaden [their] feelings in order to perform the job well," and to
"distance [themselves] from all emotions" (Bouza, 1990. p. 74).

> A police officer learns to build up a resistance to the blood and gore that intrudes
> into his or her life. You stand around at the scene of a crime puffing on cigars,
> making jokes, laughing a little too loudly. Sometimes you make jokes about
> the corpse. It is a way of ensuring that you don't become emotionally tied
> to that individual. Human pain and suffering can take over the mind easier
> than almost anything else. So we know all the tricks. Have to. Otherwise
> we'd go and blow our brains out. (Gates, 1992, p. 154)

They therefore tend toward emotional isolation and a cynically jaun-
diced view of human nature and the examples of it with which they regularly
deal. Cops, however, are proudly inclined to think of themselves, on the
other hand, as different, to feel "they're on the side of the angels," as
Bouza said (1990, p. 75), good guys, all-in-all, and a superior class. They
do "important work," Bouza pointed out, and know it. Moreover, dispassionate, even cynical, crime-fighters that they may be, cops, Bouza added,
nevertheless "feel comfortable in a service role, too" (p. 118), as the data
we reported in Chapter 10 confirm.

Working-class origins, typical patterns of recruitment, and vocationally
centered training all encourage police officers in self-identifications as
"blue-coated workers" (Reiner's [1978] term), and to a corresponding orientation toward work. Bittner (1990) has commented that a long-standing
conception of police work as a "low-grade" occupation rooted in what
he has called the "least task that could be assigned to an officer," together
with the militarization of police departments, give little inducement for
anybody to join who thought he or she could do better. He has long complained of what he sees as a failure by police to keep up with the general
upgrading of occupations in modern times, noting that the vested interests
of incumbent officers encourage resistance to it.

Monkkonen (1981), too, has remarked on the persistence of a working-
class culture among police in the United States. However, as Bittner has
also observed (1990), it may well be that a middle-class background would
not help police officers in dealing with the working-class persons who
compose the bulk of their clientele (and this same premise supports the

argument for getting more blacks into policing). In any case, Imwald and Kenney (1989) remarked on the lack of clear selection standards for police recruitment; Eskridge (1989) noted that college degrees are not often required for hiring (which cannot be surprising when most things that are learned in college are of little use in orthodox police work anyway); and McLaughlin and Bing (1989) commented on the variable character of the content, length, and quality of police training throughout the United States and its tendency toward the elementary. (Police training generally tends to concentrate on firearms, investigation, and other vocation-specific skills.)

Conservative political and moral values, and conformity to customary standards, if not universal, certainly are normal in police circles. Skeptical of theories, suspicious of professors, hostile to research, and contemptuous of reform, police officers tend to be visceral, extrospective empiricists. Direct, nonreflective and kinetic realists (or fatalists), "cops complain about the pace, but they love the action . . . the power and autonomy . . . the challenging variety" of police work (Bittner, 1990, p. 84). What counts for police officers, according to Bittner (1990), is the "huff and puff of a chase," which, he said, expresses their "preference for rushing headlong into activities that produce exhilaration over those concerned with practical accomplishments of a comparatively mundane nature" (p. 374).

Policing is not as dangerous as is commonly supposed, and it is becoming less so (the number of on-duty police officers killed has steadily declined to about 70 a year and, according to a *New York Times* report of April 25, 1991, FBI statistics indicate that the likelihood of a police officer being shot, or shooting someone else, was twice as great 20 years ago as it is now). Furthermore, Bouza (1990) noted, cops have enormous backup and support if they get into trouble. Still, "an image of police work as fraught with danger remains, and is promoted by cops and their agents" (p. 77).

Whatever the statistical risks, in an environment where violence is always latent, physical courage naturally is much valued and along with it dominance. Cops are "taught to take charge in all situations" (Bouza, 1990, p. 78). They admire gutsy responses to challenge, and "anticipating future tests, cannot allow [their] bluff to be called" (Kerstetter, 1985, p. 154). A need to preserve authority thus dominates the job because, as Bouza (1990) noted, "others are watching," and "nobody wants to be called a wimp when the fur starts to fly" (p. 70).

Wilson (1989) pointed out that "most of the time when an officer on patrol is summoned, by radio call or passing citizen, he or she can expect to encounter a situation in which great discretion must be exercised over matters of the utmost importance (life and death, honor and dishonor) involving frightened, drunk, quarrelsome, confused, angry, injured, evasive, or violent people" (p. 371). The officer in this situation must exert his or her authority—must take charge. The uniform and badge do not necessarily guarantee deference; the officer must "supplement and extend authority" behaviorally in order to restore and maintain order (see Kerstetter, 1985, for an informed discussion of this point).

Here, in this crucial truth about the situationally based and hence relative nature of the essential conditions of policing, is the crux of the police control problem, which we take up again at length in the second part of this book.

THE JUDGMENTAL NATURE
OF POLICE CRAFT

As craft workers, cops may perform their "or else" tasks in three different ways: They can negotiate, intimidate, or use physical action (Bittner, 1990). They vary in their individual skills and preferences for each one, as Bittner said, but they tend to believe that whatever they do, the effects of their actions almost always are temporary: The cop's job is to impose provisional solutions. Questions of causation are beyond the scope of their role. The only reasonable long-range goal for a cop on the street must be to protect an attitude of respect for authority. Also, failures by "assholes" to pass their attitude tests cannot be easily overlooked.

Policing is a discretionary world. Police organizations, as Bouza observed, are "anomalies . . . absolute dictatorship[s] where the lowest worker wields enormous power" (p. 44). Semimilitary in concept, police departments tend to organize themselves in strictly hierarchical ways, while simultaneously exhibiting incongruously weak administrative control. Commonly, their chiefs cannot even appoint their own key subordinates. A result, Bouza pointed out, is the peculiarly undisciplined character of police work on the street and a condition where chiefs cannot count on supervisors to control the actions of officers. Chief Daryl Gates, on his first viewing of the videotape of the Rodney King beating, was dismayed to see a sergeant present but doing nothing to control the situation (Gates, 1992, p. 4).

At the heart of their craft, cops need to feel free to do what their judgment indicates in particular situations and not be restricted to regulations. This, Bittner (1990) thought, is what cops are talking about when they say that outsiders do not understand policing:

> They mean that when one of them knocks on the door of a dwelling, having been sent there by the dispatcher to attend to some problem, he is in for an adventure from which he may not retreat, which may involve violence, and in which

he may not be second-guessed for taking "a five-foot jump over a four-foot ditch." (p. 375)

It is precisely this improvisational nature of police craft work that modern managerialist models of the police role would change by making it more planfully rational. In the process, they would replace traditional police culture with something else. Visions of this something else are somewhat variable, but a point-counterpoint of reformist pressures and resistance to them has been a continuous theme in police circles for decades. Its essentials, and its organizational expression, are neatly captured in Reuss-Ianni's image of a bifurcated police culture.

THE TWO CULTURES OF POLICING

What we have been calling a traditional *occupational* culture of policing corresponds generally to what Reuss-Ianni calls the "street cop" culture. She summarizes its essence in an aphoristic listing of features that she calls the "Cop's Code" (1983, pp. 13-16):

- watch out for your partner and then the rest of the guys working on that tour
- don't give up another cop
- show balls
- be aggressive when you have to, but don't be too eager
- don't get involved in anything in another guy's sector
- hold up your end of the work
- if you get caught off base, don't implicate anybody else
- make sure the other guys know if another cop is dangerous or "crazy"
- don't trust a new guy until you have checked him out
- don't tell anybody else more than they have to know, it could be bad for you and it could be bad for them
- don't talk too much or too little
- don't leave work for the next tour

The newer management cop culture, on the other hand, is a manifestation of the modern public-administration/scientific-management principles discussed at length in Chapters 3 and 4. By imposing a universal definition of good police practice based mainly on technical and economic criteria, management cops first and foremost seek to reduce the street cop's fundamental discretion in performing police work. Aiming to put policing on a fully reasoned basis, the modern managerialist project undertakes to standardize definitions of police roles in a system of rational administration and thereby end the highly situational, particularistic, and ad hoc formulations of their roles that street cops customarily construct on the fly.

How successful this rationalizing effort has been in achieving its managerialist aim is unclear, but the conflict it has loosed in the police community seemed plain to Reuss-Ianni (1983):

> Now there are two cultures which confront each other in the [police] department: a street cop culture of the good old days, working class in origin and temperament, whose members see themselves as career cops; opposed to this is a management cop culture, more middle class, whose members' education and mobility make them eligible for jobs totally outside of policing, which makes them less dependent on, and less loyal to, the street cop culture. In a sense, the management cop culture represents those police who have decided the old way of running a police department is finished. . . . They do not, like the street cops, regard community relations, for example, as "Mickey Mouse bullshit." . . . The management cop is sensitive to politics and public opinion [and so cannot be depended upon for support by the street cop]. The street cops who are still into the old ways of doing things are confused and often enraged at the apparent change in the rules of the system. So they fight back in the only way they have at their disposal, footdragging, absenteeism, and a host of similar coping mechanisms and defensive techniques. Nor is all this likely to change soon: the old and the new will continue to coexist for some time because the attitudes and values of doing things have not changed throughout the system. (pp. 121-122)

Bittner (1990) commented on some obvious methodological shortcomings of Reuss-Ianni's work (e.g., the research was done mainly in a single South Bronx precinct in New York City, it was entirely qualitative in approach, and its perspective is almost entirely that of the street cop). Nevertheless, Bittner thought Reuss-Ianni had things essentially right, descriptively at any rate. Summed up (by Bittner, see pp. 369-372), the street cop's view of the situation in contemporary police departments is more or less as follows:

1. Management cops are to blame for the loss of a "romanticized" image of internal police cohesion. Management cops have broken (or at least weakened) the bonds of police solidarity and customs of excluding outsiders that are traditional in policing. They have, in other words, consorted with the enemy.
2. Management cops have sold out. They have accepted influence from "assholes," opened recruitment (affirmative action, etc.), let in unpredictable peers, and thereby have made the street cop's job both more difficult and more dangerous.

3. Careerist management cops have caused an internal *class* conflict of opposed interests and hence are not only non-solidary but unreliable as well.
4. Along with an influx of "civilians" into management positions, management cops are responsible for introducing into the police world a ponderous, alien, resented management structure and with it strange, incomprehensible and off-putting stylistic differences; and they have unilaterally changed the conditions of the street cop's employment: they have "civilianized" positions that often before were those to which cops could "retire" when they could not work the streets any longer (which had the important side-benefit of ensuring that there were people in those positions on whom other street cops could rely).

Bittner commented that Reuss-Ianni herself had said little about the management-side perspective on these matters, but he allowed that it is pretty well known:

5. Management cops see the street cops' disaffection simply as resistance to reform and innovation (which in a descriptive sense probably is true) born of self-interest (which would seem inevitable, of course, if street cops believe, as suggested [earlier], that a basic moral and psychological contract has been violated by management cops).
6. The street cop's persistent resistance to police reform and administrative technologies derived from the reform movement are the cause of the pervasive estrangement between management and the police rank and file.

Thus the schism in police departments between line and administration highlighted by Reuss-Ianni's two cultures idea can be understood as resulting from an institutional collision between an established *occupational* culture of policing, with the street cop as its protagonist, and contemporary *social and political forces*, embodied by the management cop, that aim to change it (abetted in their efforts no doubt by resource scarcities, social reforms such as affirmative action initiatives, and increasing general emphases on public agency accountability and productivity).

The proximal organizational consequence of this cultural collision has been disintegration of the old unitary organic department: conflicting beliefs, values, and interests; difficulty communicating and integrating departmental policies and activities; displacement of quasi-familial relationships (and their implication of unconditional reciprocal loyalty and regard) by impersonally instrumental and quasi-contractual ones; and a suspicious, hostile, cynical, and more or less alienated work force.

The street cop's implicit strategy for waging a "culture war" has been to conserve traditional street-cop norms and values by isolating and containing the spread of management-cop culture and thereby minimizing its effects on the actual practices of day-to-day police work. The principles according to which this conservative strategy is played out, Reuss-Ianni captured in a set of street-cop precepts for dealing with the management cop's culture (see pp. 15-16). Together, they carry the strong and cynical aroma of the alienated laborer:

- protect your ass (it's every man for himself now)
- don't make waves (don't mess with the system, it might bite back)
- don't give them too much activity (they'll just come to expect it)
- keep out of the way of any boss from outside your precinct (avoid the unknown)
- don't look for favors just for yourself (no "sucking up")
- don't take on the patrol sergeant by yourself (you need a united front)
- know your bosses (their expectations), and know who's working your tour
- don't do bosses' work for them
- don't trust bosses to look out for your interests

In his review of her book, Bittner complained that Reuss-Ianni's treatment of policing was "remarkable" in reference to "occupational technique or method," in the broadest sense: mentioning "this or that procedure," but otherwise making policing look "more like an adventure than work" (p. 374). Reuss-Ianni did not talk much about what Bittner thinks of as "workmanship" (what he calls "methodical police work") and the "know-how" in dealing with situations that indicates "craftsmanship."

Cops themselves, Bittner believes, do not much value methodical police work, preferring instead the "huff and puff of the chase." They want to feel free to do what their judgment indicates in particular situations, to be free to take that five-foot leap and not be hemmed in by regulations. All this makes a good deal of sense to Bittner (1990):

> so long as one adheres to the view that policing is essentially a sequence of adventurous encounters with evil by officers or pairs of officers, who are for the most part left to depend on their own strength, courage, and wit in critical situations, interrupted by stretches of banality and boredom. But this is certainly not the only tenable view. The idea that policing is not, or at least not primarily, a quasi-military adventure has already taken hold in the minds of many police officials and has led to the introduction of demands for a higher level of social and psychological sophistication on the part of officers than has been expected in the past. (pp. 375-376)

The idea that police work is not an adventure is a management cop's thesis, of course. The problem of converting street cops to this orientation, Bittner has seen as one of creating the craftsmanship that he believes has not been of interest in traditional police culture. Street cops themselves probably also see the problem as a matter of craft. However, they also probably see themselves as already skilled in their craft. Street cops believe (surely correctly) that Bittner and others of similar persuasion are out to *re*define the craft of police work and hence its skill requirements and conditions of practice, and they are distrustful of that.

Bittner's great concern is for upgrading police and police work—putting it on a "fully reasoned basis." Like many others, he sees the current system of police organization and regulation as an impediment to police responsibility, because, as things are now, such responsibility simply will not be recognized or rewarded: "Far from providing adequate disciplinary control over patent misconduct, the existing organizational structures encourage bad police work" (p. 263). Bittner, of course, has believed that the problem of "bad police work" is rooted in a misdefinition of the police mission as criminal law enforcement, which is "merely an incidental and derivative part of police work."

Street cops and Reuss-Ianni view the situation differently. They tend to see the problem as one where "well-intentioned but overeager police managers have sought to intervene in police work through replacement rather than adaptation" (p. 122)—that is, to transform it rather than to encourage its organic evolution. Consequently:

There is the quality of a game to the present relationship between street cop culture and management cop culture. The headquarters managers can mandate MBO [management by objectives] or any planning model but they cannot make street cop/workers treat the new program seriously or honestly. The street cops, on the other hand, can and do fight back with the traditional weapons of alienated employees—foot dragging, sabotage and stealing company time. If the managers do not have the power to require serious acceptance of the planning model, neither do the workers have the power to outwit the managers altogether. What occurs is described by cops as everything from a charade to a race between a three-legged horse and a crippled kangaroo, but in any event, it's all a game. With their perception that not even headquarters took MBO seriously and that everybody knew that it was an "exercise," what happened is predictable. The response is a further attempt to maneuver for position in the contest. Dumping tickets, passing around arrests to whoever needs to "get on the sheet," breaking the picture tube on a stolen TV set, are means of circumventing the formal rules of the game, as are the responses, "You want numbers, we'll give you numbers. You want to treat us like kids, try and catch us." Also, "Why should we make you look good, what does it get us?" These clearly denote that while most of them know they cannot [possibly] win the game, they still want to seek some small victory on the way down.

12

Summary and Conclusion

We have covered a lot of ground in this discussion of the modernization of policing in America. A clear picture has emerged of contests of power: of police roles, operations, and organizations as being dynamic ideological, conceptual, and behavioral phenomena forming interactively within sociopolitical networks of interested individual and institutional actors—networks that resemble one or another variation on what Mintzberg (1983) terms a *political arena.*

The picture is not, however, a simple one of the external control of an organization. Instead, an accommodative process, albeit reluctant, is revealed in the long-term movement of police organizations toward a kind of conformity to the rationalist norms of modern society. A police chief is the institutional actor at the nexus of police tradition and antagonistic external interests. More or less influential individually, the chief is, in any case, a reference point for organizing the complex processes by which the principles of police legitimacy and modes of their expression are socially constructed.

The political arena is a metaphor for this complex process—in effect, for a process of institutionalization. Formed when an "existing order is challenged because of a change in a fundamental condition of the organization —[here in the shape of institutional pressures toward modernization]— [with attendant] breakdowns of the established order of power" (Mintzberg, 1983, p. 420), a political arena is associated with disorder, conflict, and uncertain outcomes. Regarding the police, outcomes are uncertain in their particulars, no doubt; but Murphy (1977) surely was right in forecasting that

> the future of police work may depend somewhat less on the competence and vision of the commissioner or chief. As the demonstration of police ineffectiveness and inefficiency continues, the power of the head of the police will decline, and in the vacuum the city council, the mayor, the city manager, or the budget director will be swept in to take control or have substantial leverage over deployment, budget, manpower levels, and planning.... At the same time,

from below, militant police unions will grow in strength and size to the point where any significant change in departmental policy may be subject to union veto. (p. 268)

Obviously, Murphy is speaking of more than simple direct control over the observable facts of policing. The contest is over *hearts and minds*— the undergirding concepts and tacit beliefs in which concrete actions are grounded. Further attenuation of the police chief's authority seems inevitable. Indeed, we have seen that already it is much reduced. Power over the police is being diffused both externally and internally. It is likely to become more so. However, the real winner in the contest we have been viewing will be the impersonal normative forces that are reshaping police agencies. In fact, if Murphy is right about union growth, and, as we have seen, all indications are that he is, then, despite its sometimes rebellious rhetoric and confrontational tactics, the police rank and file already is co-opted to the overarching mythology, if only by virtue of its implicit commitment to contractual modes of association and their rationalist-bureaucratic premises.

Thus by gradual institutional usurpation, an old order of policing has been passing. In the contentious procedural environments of particular police organizations, however, much is left to settle about the new order. This is considered in more detail in Part II.

Into the Political Arena:
Organizational Analysis

13

Introduction

In the first part of this book, we reviewed the societal contexts of contemporary American policing and their bearing on police leadership. We portrayed a progressive rationalist modernization of police institutions and directed attention to the actors and the interests that have been engaged or challenged by it. Focusing as we did on alterations of norms and attitudes by broad institutional forces, our analysis in Part I naturally corresponded roughly to the kinds of treatments of societal tendencies that Granovetter and Tilly (1988) associate with modernization theorists.

With these analyses as context, in this second segment of the book, we concentrate more on the local organizational implications of our institutional analysis and thereby move closer to what Granovetter and Tilly describe as analyses of "political economy." Working from the perspective of the political arena metaphor introduced in Chapter 12, and using case material from previous research in police departments, we concentrate on the interactions among particular actors (or classes of them) exercising power in particular organizational settings. We begin in Chapter 14 with a general review of the nature of power and the introduction of concepts for its discussion, starting with Mintzberg's. In Chapter 15, we enter into a more detailed consideration of the political arena, describing some illustrative cases of it and certain other power configurations. Then, in Chapter 16, we discuss these cases in relation to the dynamics of power and the management of conflict in organizations. We conclude in the final chapters (17 through 21) by revisiting the culture of policing, discussing new approaches to defining and managing police work, and commenting on the leadership challenges they pose for police administrators.

14

The Nature of Power in Organizations

Social-psychological perspectives on power and its definition are numerous (Kipnis, 1976; Pfeffer, 1992). Mintzberg (1983) defines it simply (and unexceptionally) as "the capacity to effect (or affect) organizational outcomes" (p. 4). He treats its use, the "power game," in terms of change. Borrowing Hirschman's (1970) concepts of *exit, voice,* and *loyalty,* Mintzberg suggests that neither those participants who simply accept an organizational status quo and stick around (i.e., those who opt for *loyalty*), nor those who reject a status quo and leave (i.e., those who choose *exit*) can act as "influencers" of an organization in question. Only those actors who choose *voice*— those who stay and fight—can be organizationally powerful. Mintzberg quotes Hirschman on the point, as follows:

> To resort to voice . . . is for the [client] or member to make an attempt at changing the practices, policies, and outputs of the [organization] from which one [receives services] or of the organization to which one belongs. Voice is . . . any attempt at all to change . . . an objectionable state of affairs. (1983, p. 23)

However, voice may be a choice of actors who wish to conserve an organization, as well as of those interested in its transformation. That is, voice may be chosen by actors (e.g., street cops) who prefer neither to accept changes in an organization nor to leave it, but who instead prefer literally to stay and fight in whatever ways they can. In any case, for it or against it, change or its prospect is the crux of the matter.

USING POWER, OR THE POWER GAME

A *power game,* Mintzberg submits, arises when a challenge to an existing order—call to mind the management cop challenge to street cop culture—

politicizes an organization, leaving it, so to speak, voice- or conflict-ridden: an arena for contests between contending forces for change and for preservation of a traditional status quo. Contemporary American police departments are our case in point, and in Chapter 15, we describe several cases from police venues that illustrate their power games and the players in them.

Players in Power Games and the Sources of Their Power

A particular actor's role in a power game can be described in terms of *decision rights:* that is, entitlements to participate in decision making within some (perhaps limited) domain and thereby gain opportunities to effect (or affect) organizational choices and outcomes. Mintzberg groups the players having decision rights in a power game (e.g., the "rosters of actors" we described in Part I) into two grand domains or coalitions, the one internal to the organization, the other external to it. (*Coalitions* are simply combinations of actors having permanent or temporary interests or stakes in some domain of action: police union members, alliances of chiefs with political parties, collaborations of police rank and file with command officers or with citizens, etc.)

Members of an organization's *internal coalition* assert direct influence on its decisions, in accordance with their rights in the matter. Mintzberg includes employees of all types in this internal coalition. He also includes an organization's *ideology* as part of its internal coalition: that is, that distinctive set of beliefs and values (or culture), which, like the "Cop's Code" perhaps, is shared within the coalition and steadily constrains its choices and actions.

An organization's *external coalition* encompasses all other domains and actors who assert their influence indirectly. As we have done, Mintzberg classifies unions as external influencers because, while unions involve members of an organization, their influence on the organization itself usually is exerted by means outside the organization's regular decision-making and action-taking channels. (By the same token, under certain conditions, nonemployees—mayors, citizen review boards—may act as quasi-internal influencers, directly imposing decisions on an organization, as when a mayor or city manager mandates some action or fires a police chief.)

Power Positions and Decision Rights in the Power Game

How and whether actors can support claims to decision rights within either coalition depends on their *power positions.* These depend on the resources they control: tangible things such as money, but also technical skills, knowledge, and such intangibles as legal prerogatives and connections (i.e., access to resource controllers).

Obviously, the wider the scope of an actor's (e.g., a police chief's) decision rights, the greater that actor's prospective influence. However, effective influence also depends on the skill and determination with which actors exercise whatever rights they have. Success in a power game results from using a power position with skillful persistence, and the ability to sustain effective partisanship has proven to be a particular strength of police unions (Magenau & Hunt, 1989).

In theory, a power position can be identified for each actor in the roster of actors sketched in Chapter 7 (or in any other social network). That position would be a function of each actor's comparative access to valuable resources: activity (energy and skill), money, information, symbols, sentiment, and the rest. Keenoy (1981) groups these varied resources into three types: political, economic, and actor "cohesion." Differential access to any of these resources affects the relative power positions of the various members of organizations. Take the cases of police administrators and rank and file.

Police administrators, being themselves organizational instruments of government, have direct (if variable) connection to *political* power structures. In addition, they command departmental public relations machinery and the symbols of legitimate authority. All of this helps them influence public opinion and elicit partisan support for their ideas about police work. Upon his accession to office, the former Los Angeles Chief, Daryl Gates (1992), for example, while insisting on viewing himself as nonpolitical, nevertheless, like his mentor in Los Angeles, Chief William Parker, adopted a very public policy designed, as he put it, "to build a base of support":

> I went before every conceivable group. I talked morning, noon, and night. Because I had the advantage of TV, which [Parker] didn't, I accepted all requests for interviews. In my efforts to build a strong power base, I also had meetings with people in the community. I invited CEOs from major corporations to Parker Center, offered them coffee and gave them an insider's view of the department (although not any inside information). (p. 179)

Meanwhile, diverse and unfocused, the *un*organized rank and file is weak on most political counts. When organized, however, their access to political power and ability to mobilize partisanship (Gamson, 1968) can be much increased, as we have documented in Part I and discuss again here soon.

The key to *economic* power (in the present context) is access to a supply of labor. In an open market, clearly, the police rank and file is weak; but it may be substantially stronger in a regulated one, depending on how it is regulated, of course—by themselves or by others. In one department we studied, for example, the collective bargaining agreement contained a "safety manning" clause that required every authorized position there actually to be filled, which greatly limited the department's (and the legislature's) discretion in staffing the department. When, on the other hand, police executives or city managers can refuse to fill vacancies and/or can draw on alternatives to a normal stock of police labor (e.g., computers, civilian employees, volunteers), administrative economic power obviously is increased.

An ability to determine the definition and allocation of work tasks (e.g., via the "mobile digital terminals" we mentioned earlier), or conversely, the extent of patrol officers' discretionary control of their work processes, is another economic power resource; and control of a system of standard setting, evaluation, and reward or punishment for job performance works the same way.

Meanwhile, *cohesion* (solidarity) is a power resource that affects an actor's ability to concentrate partisanship and sustain influence attempts, which is so important to effective power. As we have seen, solidarity tends gen- erally to be strong among the police. Among other things, solidarity signifies and contributes to ideological convergence, to discrimination of special interests, to perceptions of common fate (we are in this together), to procedural consensus, and to operational discipline (when everyone knows the right thing to do—whether or not others agree that it is right).

Organization of the rank and file obviously augments access to this power base. It also affords a useful way of diffusing responsibility that safeguards individual dissidents who would otherwise be separately vulnerable. Union leaders, for instance, can act not as individuals but as collective agents speaking on behalf of their constituents. Furthermore, cohesion provides a framework of sentiment for leadership and collective action and a controlled structure for external relations. This was a lesson quickly learned by minority police officers, who either were shut out of or lacked influence in white-dominated police fraternal organizations and unions. Consequently, as Dulaney (1984) found, they formed their own (the Guardians, NOBLE, and others).

For a number of reasons (not least of which is the highly decentralized and locally politicized character of American police organization), cohesion is a resource police administrators must find it hard to come by or to affect, at least when they stand in opposition to traditional police culture, which is to say, when they are anything other than regular guys or cops' cops—as Chief Gates observed, police officers "want a chief who stands up" (1992, p. 179), which, of course, he tried consistently to do. The management cop's general disability in respect to cohesion is aggravated by commonly short tenures in office: on the average, less than 3 years.

PLAYING THE POWER GAME

The actual use of power by particular players has both strategic and tactical sides. Individuals have a natural interest in controlling the models that prescribe and justify their functions and actions. An ability to set the rules of any game is plainly a major advantage in playing and winning it. Hence, participants have a *strategic* interest in what Keenoy refers to as the "ideational" aspects of social exchange: defining the rules of the game, determining the "imagery" of policing, and generally controlling the ideas and structures that govern their fate.

It is precisely this strategic interest that is at stake in the street-cop/ management-cop confrontation described in Part I. That confrontation translates into a practical interest by those involved in maximizing their relative power positions by increasing their own access to power resources (or giving the appearance of it) and/or decreasing that of others, just the way Reuss-Ianni described street cops defensively striving to isolate and weaken the management-cop culture, hoping thereby to dissipate its practical effects.

How power strategies are carried out—the *tactics* of power use—often is complicated. Among chiefs, we have noted Daryl Gates's tactics for building a power base among influential persons in the Los Angeles community. We noted, too, his promotion of an image of himself in the LAPD as a stand-up cop who backs up the men. In his 1992 book, *Chief,* Daryl Gates describes numerous ways in which he strove to demonstrate his street-cop bona fides, his identification with the rank and file, and his role as warrior-leader (appearing often in uniform, participating in police operations, personally making arrests, being among the first to visit families of officers killed or seriously injured in the line of duty, to name just a few).

More basically, however, to outsiders, Gates invariably sought to enhance the status and polish the image of the LAPD as the premier police agency anywhere in the world, one that had nothing to learn from others and neither needed nor could brook outside interference. Meanwhile, working on the inside, he undertook to forge a closed, tightly knit and special society of elites; and, in both internal and external cases, strove to promote an identification of the LAPD with the person of Daryl Gates.

Among the rank and file, power tactics commonly feature the use of calculative power equalization techniques: gambits to reduce (and sometimes reverse) the usual structural disparities of power in organizations, such as by organizing (unionization); "display" behavior (shows of force such as rallies, threats of strikes, outbreaks of the "blue flu," "ticket blitzes"); and "wrapping oneself in the flag" (or, as the police often do, raising the specters of "life and death" and crime in the street, thereby raising the "costs" of opposition).

Emerson (1962) has described four basic tactical "balancing operations" that people use to equalize power in their social exchanges. They can, he says, (a) withdraw from the relationship (by quitting, obviously, but also by staying and withholding contributions or commitments); (b) cultivate alternative sources of supply (hire civilians and auxiliaries, contract for services); (c) increase reciprocal dependence by providing another party with some good or service (do favors, give information, keep secrets); and (d) coerce the other actor (threaten firing or undesirable assignments, work-to-rule, divulge secrets).

A fifth balancing operation that probably is the most important tactic in labor relations is *coalition building* to enhance a power position and thus mitigate inequality (Keenoy, 1981). It is, of course, basic to unionization. However, coalition building has general utility, as Chief Gates implicitly recognized in his coalition-building efforts within the LAPD. It contributes greatly to cohesion as well as access to other power resources; and it also enhances actors' ability forcefully to employ Emerson's other four balancing operations, both internally and vis-à-vis outsiders.

Emerson's four tactical balancing operations may themselves be used in negotiating coalitions, either in local settings or transorganizationally. Rather like those of Chief Gates in Los Angeles, in his study of police management-union relations, Halpern (1974) described other managerial "co-optational" efforts that had a coalitional quality; and so do certain features of the movement to professionalize the police, which we discussed in Part I (see also Geller, 1985). The idea is to find something for everybody, so they all can support some idea or policy or person, at least in principle. Implementation of the police modernization program that we described earlier, for example, depended on funding from a bond issue that required voter approval. Despite a good deal of internal police opposition to aspects of the plan, a concerted attempt by the police leadership to co-opt the rank and file to support of the program (and the bond issue) largely succeeded by showing "what was in it for them." Cooperation between the rank and file and the police leaders in support of the bond issue contributed heavily to its eventual approval by the voters.

Recognition among actors of convergences of values and mutuality of interest in continuation of a relationship is a fundamental guarantee of continued interdependence and cooperation. Hence, it is a major limitation on the exercise of unilateral power. (When commitment to organizational survival and maintenance of exchange is missing, however, or when actors are unable to anticipate the consequences of actions—conditions likely to prevail in the political arenas we discuss later—this constraint may be un- reliable, and people may engage in what seem to be perversely self-defeating actions, as when the chief we earlier described received a "no" in answer to his demand of his city manager that he be allowed to run his department, or when unions knowingly vote for strikes that doom their jobs).

Coalitions illustrate an important phenomenon—the equipotentiality of power tactics—the same power tactic can serve different strategies, at least up to a point. Coalitions, and organizing activity generally, can develop and persist among actors having quite different strategic agendas. Thus important *strategic* differences may exist in the face of (and be masked by) substantial agreement among various parties on *tactical* aspects of policing and means of enhancing the status of the police. For example, provisions for a specialized police academy, more time allotted for preservice and in-service training, nationwide recruiting and higher educational requirements for new recruits, community-oriented police procedures, and objective examinations for selection and promotion of officers may not generate strong disagreement among the various parties in police departments, quite the opposite perhaps. Nevertheless, competing strategic models of policing, albeit tacit, may still be near the center of contests among partisans for control of the police agency; and it is likely that the implicit models of policing favored by different parties will be in the interest of increasing their power vis-à-vis others.

Take one especially noteworthy example. Virtually everybody, unions and police chiefs, police reformers and defenders of the status quo, politicians and the press, all talk about professionalizing the police. It is not clear at all, however, that everybody who favors "professionalization" of the police has the same interests or means the same thing by "professional." Egon Bittner (1990), an academic, for instance, is concerned with the problem of cops keeping secrets, which he views as one of the basic impediments to putting policing on a "fully reasoned basis," mainly because it precludes the development of organizational information systems on which to ground police strategies and decision making. He attributes the problem to customary bureaucratic definitions of the police officer as a "small cog in a large quasi-military machine" (p. 153).

As a model for a professional police future, Bittner talks about medicine and nursing as "elaborate and highly sophisticated" discretionary crafts. He emphasizes that they have been so for centuries, long before they commanded any "firmly formulated body of information and technique." The basis of their professionalism was their "methodically informed craftsmanship" (p. 156). In this context, Bittner talks about moving toward the "professional" accreditation of cops as "police practitioners."

The idea of "methodical police work" is basic to Bittner's image of the police officer as a practitioner of "professional, purposeful, and responsible police work" (p. 173). He stresses two features of methodical police work. The first is information management (e.g., of what he terms "area knowledge"). Like Wilson and Kelling (1982), Bittner's goal is to fashion police work as an exercise in problem-oriented discretion rather than incident-driven routine. He accepts that police work is inevitably a situated action system but argues that it needs *ethnographic* knowledge to support its effective performance: that is, a codified understanding of particular places and their peoples—the objects/beneficiaries and venues of police work. "Study and guided experience" are, therefore, needed in order for police officers to develop ethnographic observational and analytic skills. Furthermore, if area knowledge is to be organizationally valuable, it must be shared and systematized such that individual cops become the "eyes and ears of their departments," the primary sources of actionable data for their departments (p. 177).

The other feature of methodical police work that Bittner discusses is a category of "technical concerns." He envisages cops treating crime as a technical challenge, focusing on crime "problems," not so much as singular cases, but as instances of general classes (e.g., on the phenomenon of shoplifting, not on particular cases of it). The purpose of the police then becomes somewhat more abstract—less a matter of solving specific crimes, more a matter of controlling general types of them. What Bittner wants is for cops to think about what they do, to convert police work from the visceral to the cerebral ("wits over brawn"), from the reactive (incident-driven) to the proactive (problem-oriented), from the model of Dirty Harry to that of Sherlock Holmes.

In the meantime, the President of the IUPA, Robert Kleismet (1985) sees this matter of police professionalism as problematic largely because of the equation of police work with law enforcement, which he views as being only a small part of the total responsibility of the patrol officer. He, like Bittner, stresses an image of police work as a discretionary exercise of *professional* judgment, insisting that the "essence" of good policing is the "intelligent and skillful use of discretion" (p. 243). In Kleismet's view, the idea of "police as crime fighters who enforce the law in an evenhanded way without use of discretion . . . demeaned the skill of police officers" (p. 244). Also like Bittner, Kleismet endorses an order-maintenance emphasis similar to that of Wilson and Kelling (1982). *Patrol* cops, Kleismet stresses, know "what and where community problems are" and "have some sense of what works, where, and when." He, therefore, urges police executives to listen to and consult with the rank and file, and to think of them as partners. He does not, however, talk about methodical police work.

Kleismet is generally content that cops already are skilled. His agenda certainly does not preclude training, but it is not one that envisages heroic transformation of police work (although he would probably think "police practitioner" has a nice ring to it and should have some cash value, as it certainly has had for physicians). Kleismet's view of "professionalization" and culture change is, in Reuss-Ianni's terminology, an incremental adaptive one: a matter of the organic development of police practice. Bittner, wanting to put policing on a fully reasoned basis, at least by implication, leans more to the style Reuss-Ianni called "replacement"; in other words, toward a more radical transformation of police work and its purposes.

A major source of intraorganizational conflict in the police case has been the institutional change on which we focused in Part I, with the police chief as its agent and the rank and file its ostensible adversary. The resulting power game has heavily implicated police unions because, in practice, the essential conflict is a struggle for decision rights between the chief and the rank and file. This may not be true in every instance of police conflict, of course. Certainly, other issues and parties (mayors and city managers, business groups, the media, etc.) often enter the arena (see Geller, 1985), but, after the chiefs, unions generally have been the most vocal players of the police power game.

Argument has been rife on the role and legitimacy of police labor unions. On the one hand, they have been seen as usurpers of the chain of command and dangers to public order, and, on the other hand, as a primary source of stability and professionalism in American policing (see, Geller, 1985, Part 6). In Chapters 9 and 10, we discussed these matters at length and reviewed some of the literature on the subject. We described tendencies toward increasingly militant unionist orientations by police officers, together with indications of combinations by rank-and-file officers to limit both the command discretion of police leaders and their autonomy in policymaking. We also noted indications of increasingly direct public policy involvement by police associations, together with a net transfer of power from police administrators to unions via collective bargaining (see Geller, 1985, too, especially pp. 239-240).

Despite the foregoing observations, we also failed to find any empirical evidence that police unions have a major impact on actual definition of the police role in society, although we did find that members of unionized departments described themselves as experiencing more satisfaction from their police work, including their community relations, than did their nonunion counterparts. Finally, but importantly, we reported suggestions that relations among the several actors within the police agency (e.g., chiefs and the rank and file) and between these actors and the police-community network may be adversarial or cooperative, depending on the circumstances.

For example, in a case we mentioned earlier, after persuading the rank and file to play a major part in securing passage of a city bond issue crucial to departmental modernization plans, the police chief's constant stress on community relations and police services "drove the crime fighters up the wall," contributed to adversarial upheavals in the department, and eventually led the rank and file to resist implementation of many of the modernization plan's operational features. The resulting conflicts contributed to the chief's eventually leaving the department and thus departing the political arena.

15

The Political Arena

In Part I, we described a traditional theory of police chiefdom—that of the craft master (or warrior leader)—and we set this theory against a newer cosmopolitan model of the chief as public administrator. Reuss-Ianni's (1983) distinction between street-cop and management-cop models of policing is much the same, albeit hers is a more colorful terminology. In any case, the tensions between these two competing institutional myths, and their (often ambiguous) manifestations in the persons of individual chiefs, form the basis of power struggles and the specifically organizational conflicts that emerge in particular settings. We concluded that the consequences of these contests often resemble organizational power configurations of a kind that Henry Mintzberg (1983) has called "political arenas," with the figure of the police chief usually positioned uneasily at their center.

Political arena is a term from the vernacular to which Mintzberg (1983) gave technical meaning, to describe one of six basic organizational power configurations.[1] Characterized by what he calls a divided "external coalition," a politicized "internal coalition," conflicts (mainly regarding claims to decision rights) between as well as within the two coalitions, and unstable goals (as many goals as there are influencers), the concept of the political arena broadly typifies a currently common state of American policing.

VARIETIES OF POLITICAL ARENA

Mintzberg recognizes four main varieties of political arena, distinguishing among them on the basis of the intensity, the pervasiveness, and the duration of the conflicts they encompass. *Confrontation* probably is the most common of the four varieties. It is one where situationally based conflict is intense but is confined and brief. Although drawn out a bit because of the special feature of the chief's tenure in Los Angeles (it was next to impossible for elected officials to remove him), the dramatic circumstances of the LAPD in the period following the notorious Rodney King episode are a fair example of a confrontational variety of political arena, which almost certainly cost Chief Daryl Gates his job, despite his disclaimer in the last words of his 1992 autobiography that "I had stayed as long as I cared to. No one had run me out" (p. 356).

A *shaky alliance,* which may be a sequel to confrontation, is an arena in which conflict is pervasive but is somehow moderated and more or less stabilized by loose accords within the network of influencers. At this writing, the situation in Los Angeles under Daryl Gates's successor from Philadelphia, Willie L. Williams, approximates a shaky alliance. As reported in the *New York Times* (April 17, 1992, p. A18), Williams spoke to the community (the external coalition) about "healing the wounds" caused by the videotaped beating of King and, in addition, supported changes in the tenure of police chiefs in Los Angeles (a post-King investigative commission recommended giving the mayor and city council hire/fire power, and limiting chief's terms to 10 years—both of which provisions were opposed by Gates and by the LAPD's union). At the same time, Williams spoke to the rank and file (the internal coalition), resentful of the naming of an outsider as chief (the first in over 40 years), saying he wanted to restore its damaged morale, and that "too many officers have been painted with that broad brush of misconduct from the actions of a few."

A *politicized organization* is a third kind of political arena where conflict is pervasive but muted and therefore tolerable for an extended period. During this time, however, the organization's viability is likely to depend on some kind of external support. This form of political arena is a commonplace in American policing, maybe a virtual status quo, in fact. The intensity of endemic conflict, much of it associated with the impersonal institutional phenomena highlighted in this book, periodically ebbs and flows with particular local circumstances but normally stays within manageable limits, albeit perhaps with occasional episodic eruptions, as in Los Angeles or in Fort Worth, Texas, where another videotaped police beating of a man in custody led to calls for the chief's resignation. (He declined.)

Finally, the *complete political arena* represents a commonly terminal organizational state in which conflict is out of control: intense, pervasive, and brief. It would be hard to find real domestic police examples of complete political arenas, but the demise of the KGB in the Soviet Union and the Stasi in East Germany illustrate the phenomenon. In the case of police in the United States, as some cases reported later herein suggest, firing the police chief is likely to be a preferred response to the chaos of a complete political arena.

The conflicts that give rise to political arenas may occur suddenly or may develop gradually (as mostly they have in the police). In any event, however, if it is to survive, an organization must somehow moderate the intensity of the conflict it confronts and manage the dynamic power relations that generate them (see Mintzberg, 1983, Chapter 23). The ways people go about doing this, and the results of their efforts, naturally vary, depending on themselves and their circumstances.

Some extended examples of police executives dealing with conflict and power relations from varying postures in their own political environments follow. Each of the cases we describe is real, but we have given each one the name of some historical political figure in order to suggest a combination of the qualities of their individual personalities and of their particular circumstances, as well as to preserve the chiefs' anonymity, of course.

TSAR NICHOLAS

We start with a quasi-street cop, actually an elected police executive: a sheriff in a medium-sized rural western county with a large and mixed minority population. Considered a maverick by his fellow sheriffs, rather than as a political arena, really, he ran his department as a close approximation to what Mintzberg terms an *autocracy:* an organization having a passive external coalition and a highly personalized internal coalition dominated by this leader and his goals. The department's budgets were comfortable. It was modern and well equipped; and it enjoyed good community relations. Having been reelected continuously for more than 20 years, this sheriff was a fixture in the county, greatly admired by many, obviously, but detested by more than a few. We have given him the pseudonym Tsar Nicholas (the last of the Romanov emperors in Russia) to signify his autocratic ways and his status as a vanishing (if not vanished) breed.

His management style (if that is the name for it) was intensely personalized. Peremptory and frenetic, he could be an exasperating man who demanded (and got) strong personal loyalties. Much given to display behavior, he would regularly demonstrate his presence and camaraderie by bursting into meetings and, indifferent to their purposes, disrupt the proceedings with bantering conversation laced with race-related joking. The latter apparently was calculated to demonstrate what he considered his easy relations with minority officers (who greatly disliked it and kept their families from department activities because of it).

The department's structure, fluid and informal, plainly bore the sheriff's stamp. Departmental policies were marvelously inconsistent, depending almost entirely on imperiously ad hoc issue-by-issue/case-by-case determinations, as and when matters captured the sheriff's attention. Indifferent himself to disparities between nominal policies and actual practices, he, as mentioned, was regularly given to voicing what he considered "good-humored" racial slurs—despite his own policy, expressly placed in the department's policy manual, forbidding them even in jest. Cynicism about policy was understandably normal in this essentially premodern department. Although lacking a union, the department was nearly 100% civil service. Nevertheless, it was widely conceded that policy was only what the sheriff wanted, when he wanted it.

The relatively independent political status of elected police executives, such as sheriffs, no doubt presents opportunities for freewheeling administration greater than those available to most of their appointive counterparts. This is one reason why so many of the latter have little good to say about the former. (See "The Role of the Sheriff" by New York City Police Commissioner Lee P. Brown, himself a former sheriff, in Cohn [1978].) However, lest the case just described be thought to describe a peculiarly uniform state of sheriff's departments, consider next a sharply contrasting one.

GEORGE III

This is the story of a sheriff, well within the modern public administration mode of police administration, whom we have considered analogous to the heavily constrained British monarch. His was a department in a large eastern urban county, with a large minority population, and strong unionist traditions. A well-educated, well-connected, politically astute, ambitious, and careful man, this sheriff's style was moderate and distinctly managerial. His plans for his department focused on a service-delivery concept of policing, toward which he hoped gradually to move the department. He met a strong, militant, and—from his standpoint—intractable union, however, which happened also to be extremely effective as a bargaining agent and which, moreover, had a good record in minority matters.

Contractual relations between the union and the department were developed to the point where the two were essentially one body. The union was effectively the personnel bureau of the sheriff's department. No personnel procedures existed apart from the collective bargaining agreement, which dealt with such matters in exquisite detail. Personnel actions of all sorts were routinely handled via grievance procedures.

Completely thwarted in his forced institutional wedding with a powerful union, especially in personnel matters, the sheriff was able to effect few of the changes he sought in his politicized organization and soon gave up trying. He was forthright about his self-interest in this: To continue fighting, he felt, would have endangered him politically and damaged his future prospects (e.g., for higher elective or appointive office).

Unlike the first case (Tsar Nicholas), and others that follow, the power configuration here is essentially that of Mintzberg's *instrument:* a stable, bureaucratized organization dominated and controlled by its external coalition (in the form primarily of its union)—an organization that long since had completed its transition from the political arena that doubtless formed some time during its more volatile union-organizing past.

JIMMY CARTER

The experience of another public-administrative-type chief, this one appointed, was in some respects similar to the preceding one, but in a local context closer to Mintzberg's *complete political arena.* A widely known progressive police executive, this chief was a decent and able man who nevertheless failed in the specific case here described. Named chief of the police department in a West Coast city noted for high standards and innovative policies, after a nationwide search, he came on the scene as a "white knight." An intellectual who thought of himself as a liberal good guy trying to do the right thing, and as "a hell of a competent police chief," he soon found himself, as he put it, "trapped in an unending and insoluble tangle of political interests."

During his first week on the job, he spent a total of 9 hours meeting with the city's police review group, a pattern, he discovered, that would become more or less a norm. With time, he found it harder and harder to accept this situation. His problem with the board was not with the concept of civilian review as much as disappointment at this particular group's "reflexive adversary stance," and its seeming unwillingness to work for the improvement of the department.

This, together with a city manager, a city personnel chief, and other officials who seemed to look on him simply as a cop protective of a police department with which they were essentially unsympathetic, and who furthermore was something of an impediment to the expression and advancement of their own sociopolitical interests and influence, left him keenly dissatisfied and discouraged. Adding to his disaffection was the fact that white officers in the department (and some members of the community) saw him as bending over backward to favor blacks, as bypassing a court-ordered injunction against affirmative action implementation, and as generally uninterested in their welfare. The head of the department's union, meanwhile, regarded him as a politically uncritical bleeding-heart, who, in the process of trying to "do good," could do considerable damage to rank-and-file interests.

In this intensely and pervasively politicized and mistrustful environment, under constant fire from internal and external influencers, aggravated by direct interference from the city manager in departmental administration (for instance, by insisting on interviewing *all* candidates for sergeant vacancies, not just those recommended as acceptable by the chief), this chief "hated to come to work." He soon stopped—leaving for a position as something other than a police chief. His successor fared no differently and eventually "retired" from the department on medical disability. The organization, conflict-ridden as it may still be, survives, of course, apparently by periodically sacrificing its chiefs.

LYNDON BAINES JOHNSON

The preceding observations, in addition to their pertinence to the last case, pointedly introduce this one, which is the story of a man perhaps best described as a street cop cum management cop. Very well known in the police network as a progressive chief, he was a zealous reformer who had become exceptionally popular on media talk shows and was generally embraced by the press as "good cop" because of his outspokenly personal criticism of nonprogressive police administrators.

Extremely popular in his local community, a large liberal eastern city, he was equally *un*popular with the rank and file of his department, and especially with its union leaders. In the course of many events, he had succeeded in alienating virtually every uniformed faction of his department by seeking advice from civilian analysts and planners, bypassing senior officers, criticizing the productivity of officers, and a steady stream of other offenses. Eventually, he lost the regard of the city's mayor as well, largely, it can be surmised, because of the heat the chief generated and the publicity he got. (It was said that he could easily have won election as mayor but probably would not have got a hundred votes out of the police department.)

He was, at this point, invited to become chief of a department in an affluent eastern urban jurisdiction. There, he continued his articulate but highly controversial public pronouncements, and he quickly became at odds with his unionized officers generally and with minority officers in particular (who felt he was uncommitted to their cause). As his conflict with the union escalated to virtual warfare, the chief found himself an issue in the local elections, with the union supporting a candidate sympathetic to the chief's ouster, thus pretty well completing transition to a *complete political arena*. The union's candidate did win the election, and the chief was ousted. The police union was not satisfied, however. Believing the deposed chief to be inimical to the interests of police officers everywhere, it did everything it could, and with no little success, to prevent him from getting a position in police administration anywhere else.

BONAPARTE

Yet another street cop cum administrator, this one was also a reformist chief cut from some of the same cloth as the one just described, but without the same penchant for notoriety. In collaboration with the mayor of a major southern city, he had unseated his weak and administratively unskilled predecessor to take over a notoriously corrupt and racist department, through the ranks of which he had worked his way—a department where detective jobs were passed out for political favors, violence was customary, and race relations were abysmal.

A powerful personality, the new chief introduced many administrative changes and sociological programs intended to clean up and professionalize the department. He also strove to set a high moral tone, combining it with a strong faith in rational administrative methods (such as objective tests for selecting police officers).

A difficult blend of charismatic craft master (or warrior leader) and public administrator, this chief reigned successfully for a time, essentially as an "enlightened benevolent despot," over what probably is best described as a *shaky alliance* form of political arena, where conflict was muted, and loose accords existed among the centers of power. He attracted a good deal of national attention doing it and, as a result, soon left the city to become chief in a larger one. There, he found severe labor problems in a deeply politicized organization (resembling a *confrontational* variety of political arena) that culminated in an acrimonious police strike, the chief's removal from office, and his departure from the city and from police work altogether.

Labor problems had, in fact, been gathering in the shaky alliance that was his previous (nonunion) department, where they were spawned by mounting rank-and-file concerns for job security in the face of so autocratic a change agent. The chief, however, had denied the existence of any serious rank-and-file unrest, and anyway had been naively convinced that he could "handle them" and "knew how to keep a union out." Thus his legacy to his successor was a shaky alliance that was becoming shakier.

MILLARD FILLMORE

Bonaparte's successor in his first department contrasted sharply with him in personal style but also wanted to "professionalize" the department.

A man who had long been a deputy chief there, he, along with the other deputy chiefs, had been intentionally bypassed by the departed chief (who had favored direct dealings with selected junior command officers). Among the programs he inherited from the former chief was a task force that had been formed to develop antiracism programs. The new chief soon disbanded the task force, however, because it "got too much into criticism of the administration, to antagonisms, and dealt too much in personalities and criticism of the rank structure." The result, as the chief saw it, was increased "separatism" and "people had begun backing off from the committee."

The chief's alternative plan was to "move to the precinct-level and work things out there." He admitted to having no clear idea of how this would happen, except that he would get reports from the commanders and would stress that the problems were theirs and that they should develop solutions to them (and, presumably, report them).

This strategy, of course, had the attractive quality of getting the chief out of the middle. He recognized that there were significant racial problems in his department and community and was frustrated by his inability to solve them; but he wanted to intellectualize them—to deal with them in a logical way. He wanted nothing to do with the emotional aspects of racial issues, the expression of which he viewed as disruptive at best.

Well-intentioned but no less autocratic in disposition than his predecessor, this chief had the additional problem of confusing his preferences with logic. In any case, he was baffled by his inability to command the situation in his particular political arena. He felt he was "getting it from all sides," not excluding his friends of long standing (among whom were numbered some of the department's premier racists). His support from the city's mayor was tepid at most. He was getting a steady barrage of criticism from black city council members, was watching a developing union movement in his department (the one his predecessor had denied existed), and to cap it all, an intensely controversial shooting of a black woman had inflamed both the Southern Christian Leadership Conference and the Ku Klux Klan.

The fact that he was simply not an adept administrator naturally made his problems still worse. His chain of command was working poorly, and he was overwhelmed. He had hoped for magic from the task force—of a "come let us reason together" variety—but he did not get it. In the end, what he got into was training, concluding that many, maybe most, of the department's problems (including racial ones) were curable that way.

Thirteen years after the accession of these two chiefs, consensus of opinion was that neither corruption nor racism was any longer blatant, but otherwise "not much [was] different in the department." This judgment, however, overlooked the obvious progression of the department's political arena from a shaky alliance to a "politicized organization," with intensified, more pervasive, and surely more durably explicit conflict.

MICHAEL DUKAKIS

This last case is a reasonable approximation to a pure technocratic management cop. The case is set in a small midwestern city. The city once had been a "gang town rife with corruption," but in the 1950s, it reformed its government with the explicit purposes of generally professionalizing its administration and insulating the police department from political pressure—watchwords in the city still.

The police department itself was cleaned up mainly by "a tough and honest cop" who was its night commander. The subject chief, as an undergraduate student intern, had worked with this man. Afterward, he (the subject chief) took a master's degree in police administration, then worked his way through the ranks in another city, and eventually returned to the department as its chief.

Committed to a public administration conception of the police executive's role, this chief made an emphatic point of his department's being "clean, and especially nonpolitical"—and so, by and large, it was seen by most observers. Atmospherically, the department seemed decidedly low key. There was little sense of the ferment common in police agencies. The chief was an obviously bright, sophisticated, and modern professional administrator: an "enlightened bureaucrat," who stylistically might as well have been a city manager. He stated directly that he conceived his power in the community and the department to derive from his professional expertise, not from charisma or a political constituency.

Within the department, the chief was, and knew he was, widely perceived as a "prudish martinet," an image he, in fact, sought to nourish, convinced as he was that "being nice and one of the boys" defeats a chief's ability "to keep his finger on the department." Still, he thought of his managerial style as being "highly personalized"—"they never know when or where I'll pop up." (The feeling in the department was that he did not "pop up" very often anywhere.) In any case, running the department day-to-day was a deputy, a gravel-voiced no-nonsense cop. A blunt, aggressive, often-obscene man, he contrasted sharply with the chief. A past president of the police benevolent association, he was a dominating presence who was widely respected as a street cop and influential in the department. His presence in the department's number two job almost certainly helped legitimize the chief's tenure.

As the chief described them, his goals for the department were, in the main, what he thought the department already had become: disciplined, modern, technologically advanced, and "as good a department for its size as exists." He stressed the importance of setting high standards, along with his expectation of "unbiased, vigorous law enforcement." He also noted that, "although the blacks may not believe it," he wanted a service-oriented agency that provided the training to make it that way. At the same time, he spoke sympathetically of the special problems of managing people such as police and firefighters—"people who are under endemic stress, with their self-protective solidarity, and the like."

In fact, this chief attracted much attention in the national law-enforcement community, in which he was an active participant, as one of the new breed of police administrators, and a "comer." On the other hand, within the department he was seen (without hostility) as detached: "He's not here enough, he doesn't know what's going on." One of his aides described him as "aggravating and sometimes dispiriting to work for," as "stiff and cold," as a man who treats people as "pieces of the inventory," and as one who will not delegate—but also bright, innovative, and honestly progressive.

The department's manifest character, perhaps mirroring its chief, was formalized, efficiency-oriented, but low-intensity, quiescently stable, and expressive of essentially modest expectations—an organization on hold, it seemed, something close to Mintzberg's *dominated meritocracy* hybrid power configuration, focused on internal expertise, but emphasizing centralized controls on the independence of its professionals. All this, however, in a context of survey information indicating a lack of trust and con- fidence in the department's leadership: a context where, generally speaking, people "let things happen" rather than try actively to change anything; where problems were more likely to arise from errors of omission than of commission. All of this is consistent with Mintzberg's expectation that a dominated meritocracy because of its implicit usurpation of rank-and-file discretion via bureaucratization would be associated with resistance, if perhaps more muted in expression than in literal political arenas.

What these several cases teach about the dynamics of power, management, and survival in political arenas and kindred power configurations is the subject of the next chapter.

NOTE

1. Configurations are integrated concatenations of features, which, holistically, are related systematically with features of their situations (cf. Miller & Friesen, 1984).

16

Conflict, Management Styles, and the Dynamics of Power

As portrayed in the previous chapter, *Tsar Nicholas* was an essentially nonbureaucratic autocrat enjoying a "patriarchal" regime. His was a strong personality but one carrying no particular message other than an implicitly traditional one. A broadly benevolent figure, really, he was unthreatening in any basic way. Also, in any case, he worked from a strong external political base with an unorganized work force that was doing well enough materially. Integrated with or dominating both external and internal coalitions, his regime intermixed political and instrumental qualities in ways much like those of the nineteenth-century prebureaucratic police organizations (cf. Klockars, 1985; Monkkonen, 1981) that were precursors of the more modern systems exemplified by the departments described in the other cases here.

In contrast, *George III* is a rational/bureaucratic agent who operated in an already heavily bureaucratized and organized setting. An individual who had a solid external political base, but who carried no strong message of local reform, he was a careerist with a plainly instrumental view of his office. Committed mainly to personal advancement, rather than organizational change, he found himself in a disappointing but not uncomfortable, and anyway presumably temporary situation. He was therefore willing to go with a flow that seemed unthreatening to his self-interest, and which, in any case, was basically in keeping with his contractualist orientations (he was in fact a lawyer).

The third case (*Jimmy Carter*) differed markedly from either of the first two: a rational-bureaucratic reformer with no political base who walked into a complete political arena where he faced an uncooperative organized work force in an intensely and diversely politicized local environment comprising a wide range of influencers operating on many different agendas, none of which was his. In the midst of this complex of unstable alliances and institutional hostilities, which seemed to him altogether irrational, he concluded that his situation and mission were hopeless, and so he quit (fled might be more like it), it may be presumed, in order to preserve his own well-being.

In the fourth case (*Lyndon Baines Johnson [LBJ]*), we encountered another different blend of organizational features: a charismatic/moralistic reformer who carried a very strong message supercritical of traditional police models. He himself generated the confrontations that fractured the internal coalition and eventually resulted in a complete political arena in his second department. Implicitly convinced that good was necessarily on his side, he was in fact, however, an individual whose power resources actually were few in the face of a hostile organized work force and a disintegrated external coalition. His flamboyant personal style stimulated dissension and no doubt aggravated reactions to his throwing down the antitraditional gauntlet, which helps explain the extravagant response to him by the police union.

Bonaparte, the chief in the fifth case, was another charismatic figure but one less moralistically reformist or rhetorically outrageous. Bureaucratic, but autocratically rather than contractually so, he was intolerant of the dissent he exacerbated, overestimated his ability to manage it, and suffered from an exaggerated sense of his personal power. Consequently, he more or less blundered into the complete political arena in his second department, which precipitated his being ousted from his job.

His successor in his first department, *Millard Fillmore,* was a man who simply became lost in the woods, so to speak. Having no particular sense of mission or direction, he was clearly a management cop, who inherited an increasingly politicized organization. A bureaucrat in the contractualist mode, with few power resources, his goal was simply to keep the lid on. He stressed being reasonable, sought to avoid conflict, and, when it occurred, exercised management by flight. His disposition was to personalize the sources of conflict, and then to try to transform people by training them, naively hoping thereby for their enlightenment.

Finally, *Michael Dukakis* describes a near-approximation to a triumph of bureaucratic (contractualist) rationality, a "man in a gray flannel suit," a CEO. Dispassionate and by no means an *overt* change agent, this chief *embodied* the message (i.e., the institutional myth of rationalism). Although a messenger of the future, his bearing suggested no serious or obvious threat to the rank and file. Indeed, if somewhat annoying because of his detached personal style, he was institutionally innocuous precisely because his style was viewed merely as a personal characteristic and nothing more basic. Furthermore, his deputy chief, stylistically at least a classic street cop, gave his administration a satisfying aura of traditional police reality that made it easier for the department's internal coalition to live with their chief.

Viewed collectively, these cases may reveal not only a spectrum of power configurations, but also intimations of a developmental sequence: a continuum of police power structures from more autocratic forms (Tsar Nicholas) through more politicized conditions (e.g., LBJ) toward more bureaucratically stabilized instrumental and meritocratic structures (George III and Michael Dukakis). Implicit in such development is progressive, although not necessarily linear, change in the power position of the chief. A Michael Dukakis unquestionably is personally a weaker leader than a Tsar Nicholas, but he is arguably stronger than an LBJ or even a Bonaparte. Table 16.1 roughly summarizes the power positions of these seven chiefs according to Keenoy's three power bases, adding ideology.

Political arenas develop in response to conflicting demands. These may arise from a change in some fundamental condition of an organization (e.g., a new technology, or an affirmative action mandate); from a breakdown in the established order of power (as when an ideology, such as the cop's code, weakens); or when conflicting demands develop gradually from inexplicit sources, such as the tacit effects of the diffuse institutional forces we describe often in this book. Mintzberg remarks, too, that combinations of factors may be involved in the genesis of political arenas: changes in conditions that "provoke breakdown and challenge concurrently, and these two reinforce each other, in Ping-Pong fashion" (p. 437).

This Ping-Pong effect can be seen, for example, in the way Los Angeles rapidly became critical from the mutually reinforcing interactions among the circumstances of the Rodney King beating, perceptions of the police chief (whether warranted or not) as an unsympathetic racist, a seemingly cavalier acquittal by a Simi County jury of the officers involved in the beating, and a context of long-standing racial and ethnic tensions and resentments in the city.

It seems likely, too, that political arenas, in addition to having multiple reciprocating roots, may, over their life cycles, from birth through development to dissolution, take different forms episodically, as an organization responds to specific circumstances that exacerbate local conflicts (see Mintzberg, 1983, pp. 433ff.). We saw evidence of this earlier in the progression of the LAPD to a confrontational political arena and on to a shaky alliance following the King episode.

Of the several political-arena life cycles described by Mintzberg, however, the one that seems most easily to fit police organizations and their institutional conditions is his *Life Cycle 3: gradual politicization*. This is a developmental case widely observed in public agencies of all sorts, where "multiple changes in and between coalitions coupled with slow breakdown

Table 16.1 Summary of Chiefs' Power Positions

Chief	Politics	Economics	Cohesion	Ideology
Tsar Nicholas	Hi	Hi	Hi[a]	NA[b]
George III	Hi[c]	Lo[d]	Lo	Lo
LBJ	Lo	Lo	Lo	Lo
Bonaparte[e]	Hi/Lo	Hi/Lo	Hi/Lo	Mod/Lo
Jimmy Carter	Lo	Lo	Lo	?
M. Fillmore	Lo?	Lo	Lo	Lo
M. Dukakis	Mod	Hi	Mod	Hi

NOTE: "?" = uncertain; "Hi" = high; "Lo" = low; "Mod" = moderate.
[a] Due to "particularistic" relationships/control of rewards
[b] No clear ideology was implicated, but if anything, this was high on traditional grounds.
[c] Nominally high as an elected official, but effectively neutralized by union.
[d] Contractual constraints very strong, including a "manning" clause requiring all authorized positions actually to be filled.
[e] Departments 1/2 (first and second in chronology).

in legitimate power gradually lead to the politicized organization" (p. 446). The several sections of Geller's (1985) anthology on *Police Leadership in America* (i.e., "The Chief as a Major Municipal Policymaker; The Chief and the Community; . . . and the Media; . . . the Law and Lawyers; . . . the Union"), to all intents and purposes, are descriptors of the police organization's diverse set of influencers or, as we have called them in Chapter 7, its "roster of politicizing actors." The Geller book depicts both the political investiture of the police in America, and, interestingly, because many of its chapters were written by police practitioners, it demonstrates these principals' apparent acceptance of that investiture as a fact of their lives.[1]

In the long run, Mintzberg suggests, deeply politicized organizations need artificial means of support in order to survive. Well-institutionalized organizations such as police departments certainly enjoy such support and are unlikely to pass over the bar. Whatever the tumult and dissension in Los Angeles, its police department will remain, as did the department in Philadelphia, from whence Los Angeles's new chief, Willie Williams, hails. After the incredible 1985 shoot-out there with the MOVE cult and the police bombing of the building in which the cult members were holed up, which destroyed an entire city block and killed some 20 people, children among them, a reform commissioner was appointed from outside the department (who did not stay long, however) and a task-force investigation severely criticized the police and its administration. However, as Bouza (1990) observed, it soon was business as usual, as the reform chief was succeeded by an "up-from-the-ranks insider."

More likely than death in the case of politicized police departments is one or another form of organizational transformation—perhaps toward something resembling what Mintzberg calls the "dominated meritocracy." We saw an apparent approximation to this hybrid power configuration in the "Michael Dukakis" department. Generally, a dominated meritocracy is an organization whose support depends on a single external influencer (e.g., government), which encourages that influencer to exercise close control over the organization (as Los Angeles is trying to do by seeking to increase control by elected officials over its police chief's tenure).

Aptly again, Geller's (1985) volume, especially Part I, contains a pertinent discussion by three chiefs and two mayors of the entwined relations between police chiefs and municipal authorities. In his introduction to this part of the book, Geller concludes that "the chief's municipal superior needs to play a significant role in assuring quality policing" (p. 4). He hopes that this "significant role" will be played in a nonpartisan manner, but whatever its partisan character, we would expect the outcome of its playing to be a partnership emphasizing administrative/economic rationality that would foster bureaucratization of the organization (probably under the banner of professionalizing it). As we know, however, this outcome, in turn, commonly stimulates resistance (at least in the short term) from the internal coalition (the rank-and-file street cops, for instance), tends to divide the external coalition, and excites overall politicization of the system. The result is a political arena (politicized organization form) with its power struggles and conflict, and hence the fuel for further evolution, most likely, of course, in managerialist directions.

We have described only a few selected cases, to be sure; but it is nonetheless tempting to conclude from them (and other anecdotal indicators) that while "Lone Rangers" and street cops cum public administrators get famous as reformers, it is the management cops who seem to keep their jobs. Meyer and Rowan (1977) might perhaps have predicted this from their argument that organizational forms that match with their institutional environments survive, whereas those that deviate fail. Chief Daryl Gates in Los Angeles was an approximate exception to this generalization, which tends to prove the rule: His survival in Los Angeles was based heavily on an anomalous tenure arrangement that may change for his successors.

The cases also illustrate the force of arguments on the comparative advantages of chiefs who are insiders (i.e., who rise through the ranks, preferably in the same department where they become chief) versus those who are outsiders. Monkkonen (1981), as we have noted, has pointed out that police in the United States, despite many changes, have steadfastly maintained a working-class culture, which has tended both to resist upgrading and to restrict command positions to former members of the rank and file, as a means to ensuring top-level responsiveness to rank-and-file demands. Among our seven cases, ignoring the sheriffs, two (Jimmy Carter and LBJ) were outsiders; two were insiders (Millard Fillmore and Michael Dukakis); and one (Bonaparte) was a mixed case: an insider in his first department and an outsider in the second.[2] In each case where the chief was an insider, politicization of his department was less and the tenability of his position was greater than either case when the chief was an outsider.

Related to the insider-outsider issue is the posture of a chief as an explicit reformer. With the possible exception of Michael Dukakis, none of the chiefs in our examples who were frank reformers fared well: especially not those, who, like LBJ, self-righteously overestimated their moral authority. In fact, Michael Dukakis may be another exception that proves a rule. Unlike LBJ, his reformist position was only implicit and, in any case, was neither moralistic nor ideological. His style was not revolutionary, even if his message was. In effect, whether intentional or not, his methodology for changing police roles was nearer to what Reuss-Ianni called "adaptation" than the more typical reform-bent management cop's strategy of replacement. (We return again to this question of changing police roles and culture in a later chapter, when we consider at greater length the movement toward community-based policing and quality management.)

Finally, the seven cases we have described also show how tactical commonalities can mask important strategic differences in police leadership. Allowing for some variation in personal styles, George III, Bonaparte, and Michael Dukakis all display similar rational bureaucratic patterns of administration, despite their substantially different strategic orientations. The first of these men was strategically oriented mainly to advancing his personal career as a public official, the second toward personal domination of the departments over which he presided, and the third to progressive conversion of his department to a modern management *system*.

NOTES

1. See Mintzberg (1983, pp. 306-314) for summary descriptions of the various power configurations. The political envelopment of contemporary police agencies is perhaps rather more diversified than it once was in the era of local machine politics; but, in any event, the police never have been strangers to political domination (see Berman, 1987).

2. The two sheriffs are special cases because of their mode of accession to office (election). They sometimes do, but often do not, rise through the ranks of the departments they lead, although they are normally insiders, in the sense of being members of their departments' host communities. An article in the *New York Times,* while noting a number of changes in policing since the 1960s, especially in educational requirements, observes, albeit in passing, that "the new breed of chief is still usually a former patrol officer" (Andrew H. Malcolm, "Police chief's objective: Greater responsiveness," April 23, 1990: A12).

17

Power and Leadership
The Police Chief as Change Agent

Mintzberg advises that voice-ridden political arenas, despite their appearances, may yet be functional configurations—if, that is, they facilitate adaptation to changed conditions, correct previous dysfunctional changes, or (as shaky alliances) accommodate irreconcilable forces, or even if they simply speed up deserved death. Mintzberg's discussion of these adaptive matters tends to treat the situation as one of errant organizations that require correction (or demise). We have no quarrel with this theme but would raise a question as to what the standards of errancy might be.

Police departments are errant (if that is the word) not because of the "poor performance" that Mintzberg stresses, but because of changing criteria resulting from their modernization: an emphasis on impersonal rationality, standard operating procedures, specialization of functions, universal rather then particularistic norms of practice, and legal bases of authority. About these institutional matters Mintzberg says little or nothing, concentrating as he does on strictly *organizational* matters.

Our emphasis in this book, in contrast, has been on the *institutional* roots of organizational conflicts. The police chief, we have argued, functions in the contemporary American police department as an institutional as well as an organizational actor. He or she will therefore be a carrier or instrument of institutional norms, an inducer of organizational change, and, consequently, an inevitable instigator of local conflicts. This is why, structurally, American police organizations today are almost sure to resemble one or another form of political arena. Fundamental institutional battles are being waged in them. These struggles are more or less intense in particular cases, but they naturally swirl about the person of the institutional leader, the police chief.

Joe McNamara, a former New York City police officer, currently chief in San Jose, and a Harvard Ph.D., writes hard-boiled police novels that have prompted comparison with Wambaugh, Chandler, and McBain. There is not much of the management cop in his stories. In *The Blue Mirage* (1990), his detective protagonist, Fraleigh, an old-fashioned and foul-mouthed street cop, has become acting chief of his tumultuous Silicon City, California, department. His prospect of permanent appointment is highly uncertain. The story, as the book's jacket blurb puts it, is "filled with . . . tough, humorous [and raunchy] talk, nonstop realistic action, and insight into the way cops think" (or at any rate how they like to fancy their jobs).

At the book's climax, after a violently botched sting operation in which Acting Chief Fraleigh was directly involved and was wounded, he presents himself before the city council called to act on his confirmation as chief. Anticipating rejection and believing the sting to have been a fiasco by "trigger-happy Keystone cops who let one hundred sixty grand be ripped off while we blasted everyone but the thief " (p. 316), Fraleigh is startled to find the council room nearly filled with cops, some with their families. Assuming they "had all turned out to see him get canned" (p. 317), he is dumbfounded when rhythmic clapping begins, and he asks "What the hell are they clapping for?" Told the clapping is for him, in disbelief he asks, "Why?" His street cop associate, "the Block," tells him. "Because you're a dumb asshole cop just like them and this is the last chance they have to do it before you get canned" (p. 318).

To everyone's surprise, however, Fraleigh is (narrowly) confirmed. At lunch afterward with his older brother, in a restaurant that "draws the movers and shakers," he allows that he would "rather be over at the hall hoisting a few with the cops" (p. 323). In what amounts to a rite of passage from street cop to management cop, his brother counsels him, however, that now he has to be "above that sort of stuff" if he wants to be respected, that he cannot be too close with anyone, must be impartial and removed— "you're the chief. You've got to be whistle-clean."

Simply put, our argument in this volume has been that, when considered in the aggregate as *institutions,* contemporary police departments are political arenas. As distinct *organizations,* however, particular police agencies may exhibit different power configurations, depending on particular local circumstances. The seven stories told in Chapter 15 show how situational contingencies induce variations in local power configurations, while leaving still tenable simultaneous arguments about more generally uniform transformations of American police institutions.

Local conflicts arise from local conditions, clearly, but in the police, they are framed by a more nearly universal fight, which is less about who has direct control over the observable facts of policing than it is about the norms in reference to which, as Kingsley Davis (1950) has said, relations are defined and justified. Individual police chiefs' practices may be variable in their particulars, as the cases reported in Chapter 15 and elsewhere illustrate, yet they remain constant in general. They are, however, always subject to more or less continuous redefinition in social transactions. The parties to these transactions—the chiefs, the cops, the mayors, the union leaders, the academics, the citizens—not only act on the basis of personal models of their worlds, but they also seek to promote their ideas and preferences as tangible policies for others to follow and as true and proper views of things.

The principal challenge to a police chief, then, is not technical, but, if you will, spiritual. Management is important to operating any organization, of course, but the primary task of the executive is leadership: the will and ability to articulate a mission, an agenda, and a set of legitimizing values for an enterprise to which others can commit their energies (Selznick, 1957).

Power, then, consists of an individual's ability to influence, intentionally or not, the subjective models that construe the premises and justifications of others' actions. Politics is a normative contest for hearts and minds: "what is at stake is not so much the actions of men . . . , but their ideals, the moralities to which they owe their public allegiances" (Gusfield, 1963, p. 177) —the terms, in short, by which they justify their actions.

In an April 21, 1991, letter to the "op-ed" column of the *New York Times,* a police psychologist, Harvey A. Goldstein, debated the contention that better educated police forces would result in less police brutality. Goldstein agreed that education would not hurt but argued that it was organizational norms not education that bore most heavily on police brutality. Drawing on the well-known prison experiments by Zimbardo at Stanford, which had to be suspended because carefully screened college students acting in the role of guards became excessively brutal to other students acting as prisoners, Goldstein argued that in order to "impact intentional excessive force, the core values of the organization's management need to demand its extinction."

18

The Police Chief and the Culture of Policing

Many people, women and men, are attracted less to the intellectual challenges of police work than to its real and imagined macho joys. Some of these people habitually take those five-foot jumps over four-foot ditches —and a few look for four-foot ditches they can use as justifiable opportunities for taking five-foot leaps. Mostly, however, as Bouza said, the system weeds out the real brutes.

THE MANAGEMENT OF VIOLENCE

Coercion, force, and violence are inherent in police work, however, and some brutality is probably an inevitable accompaniment. Pumped up by the "huff-and-puff" of a chase, or when the adrenaline flows as a cop's authority on the street is challenged, it happens. Violence is a part of police work—part of the culture of policing. Controlling and minimizing it among all the affected parties is a constant challenge to civil society and to the police as its agent.

In Los Angeles on March 3, 1991, a remarkably large group of police officers (20 or more) beat, or looked on while their fellow officers beat, a citizen apparently guilty of no more than a traffic offense. As LAPD Chief Daryl Gates described the videotaped scene:

> As the . . . officers closed in on King, he dropped to his knees. The officers began whacking him with their batons, administering blow after blow. The man rolled on the ground as they repeatedly struck him across the legs, the back, and about the head. One officer kicked him five times. Another stomped on his head.
>
> I stared at the screen in disbelief. I played the fifty-second tape again. Then again and again, until I had viewed it twenty-five times. And still I could not believe what I was looking at. To see my officers engaged in what

appeared to be excessive force, possibly criminally excessive, to see them beat a man with their batons *fifty-six* times, to see a sergeant on scene who did nothing to seize control, was something I never dreamed I would witness. It was a very, very extreme use of force—extreme for any police department in America. (1992, pp. 3-4; emphasis in the original)

From their subsequent behavior—talking about the event on their continuously monitored patrol car communication system—it is plain, however, that these officers believed nothing much would happen as a result of their actions. How could this be? Also, what, if anything, does it say about police in America?

The easy answer to how a Rodney King episode could happen is some form of rotten-apple theory: Mr. King got beat up the way he did because he had the bad luck to come upon 4, 5, or 20 or more bad cops (one of whom happened to be a supervising sergeant). Obviously that will not wash. There is more to such episodes than a few rotten apples. The problem in Los Angeles and in many other American cities is at once bigger and more basic than rotten apples.

Certainly there are cops who are bad guys. However, there are bad guys everywhere. There are bankers who are bad guys. In fact, the police probably try harder to screen out bad guys than banks do. The real trick for any organization, however, and especially the powerful ones such as police departments, is to keep even the bad guys who get in from doing bad things. This requires organization.

More than that, it requires leadership. Two things that are true of cops on the street are that (a) they work in a world of uncertainty and danger, and (b) because of that, they have a low tolerance for defiance of their authority. Authority, more than guns and clubs, is the police officer's shield. (Mr. King's big mistake was that he ran away and was defiant, and for that he paid.)

A third truth about police officers is that, on the street, they can be only loosely supervised. This, too, follows from the uncertainty natural to their work. Despite modern attempts to rationalize and bureaucratize the police, direct administrative control remains weak. Individual police officers are largely on their own. They cannot be much regulated by rules. The situations they deal with are too variable (and sometimes volatile) for anything but the most general kinds of rules to be of any use. What they need mostly, in addition to careful selection, is training in policies, programs, and processes of policing, and above all in values (see Cohen & Feldberg [1991] for discussion and exemplification of this matter in a context of programs of ethical education for the police).

LEADERSHIP AND CULTURE

Not from Rodney King's standpoint, maybe, but surely from the public's, the most disquieting thing about his beating was not that it was willful and vicious, but that it was, in effect, sanctioned. Not sanctioned in the sense that somebody in authority, Stacey Koon, the sergeant on the scene, maybe, said, "Okay, fellas, go get this guy," but sanctioned in the sense that tolerant conditions—a system, a culture—had evolved in which, if not actually encouraged, such behavior carried little risk to the offender, as long as it did not become public at any rate. Inevitably, in such a context, occurrences such as the Rodney King incident become more likely to happen (and, sooner or later, to become public).

If, however, the problem in Los Angeles (and elsewhere) is not principally one of bad cops but of bad culture, then who or what is to blame, and what is to be done about it? Policing is, after all, the public's business. Well, the obvious place to start a responsibility watch is with the chief.

We have said that chiefs and other police administrators have only modest ability to influence the operations of their departments directly. The complexity of police work and the inherent ambiguity of police performance standards militates against it. The chief's influence is therefore largely indirect and symbolic, but in its immediate organizational context, it is substantial nonetheless.

Patrick Murphy, in his 1977 autobiography, spoke, for instance, of what he called a "semi-ecclesiastical dimension" to the police chief's job. Murphy, now an advisor to the National Council of Mayors and, anyway, someone who knows what he is talking about, offered an image of the police chief as "something akin to a secular pastor." A police chief, he said, "can be viewed not only as the community's chief law enforcement officer but also as the custodian of the community's morals. . . . the police chief becomes the focal point not only of a community's sense of physical security but even of its spiritual well-being" (pp. 56-57).

Policing, by implication, quite literally involves a "sacred trust." The police chief is the key agent for ensuring that this trust is honored. His or her most important job is to make clear what is right, what the police stand for in a community, and to act vigorously and consistently, not just in speeches, to support this vision and to cause it to become routinely manifest in police conduct. Revelations of police wrongdoing, as Murphy points out, "can shake a community to its core," as they did in Los Angeles, simply because of the violations of essential trust they entail.

A frustrated lieutenant in a semirural West Coast city once made vividly real this crucial anchoring of individual police officers' actions in moral values. Outraged by procedural encumbrances on police officers in fighting crime, by the injustices suffered by innocent victims, and by what he saw as the arrogance of professional criminals in his community, he spoke emotionally of solving the problem with measures evocative of Central American death squads, up to and including summary executions. He ended his harangue, however, by remarking that "it's a damn good thing I'm a Roman Catholic," his point being that, without a restraining faith and stabilizing moral norms, he feared for his ability to resist the temptation to abuse his power by personally meting out rough "justice" on the street.

We have insisted that there is no way around the reality that police officers must handle individual cases selectively. It is in the nature of law enforcement, peacekeeping, order maintenance, or whatever police work may be called. However, civil society must be able to trust the police officer's judgment and moderation. We have been accustomed to thinking of police departments as quasi-military command-and-control systems, but we know that this idea is illusory and misleading and, for that reason, dangerous. It implies a degree of immediate external control of working-level police officers that does not (and almost surely cannot) exist. Whatever the given theory of policing, police officer judgment and discretion reign on the street. Nor would we want it otherwise, really. We want police officers to be judicious, but we also want them to be humane in their judgments and in the ways they do their jobs.

A 1984 panel on "The Future of Policing," organized by the William O. Douglas Institute for the Study of Contemporary Social Problems in Seattle and the Edna McConnell-Clark Foundation, on which one of us (Hunt) served, together with some of America's leading police officials, police union leaders, and scholars, observed that "we can expect police leaders to give their officers discretion in enforcing the law," but we can expect them "simultaneously, to hold those officers accountable for their exercise of that discretion." However, just how is this done? How are chiefs to regulate the judgment and discretionary actions of individual officers? We know it cannot be done only or even mainly by rules or other external means. It can only be done by self-control. On the street, there is no alternative.

Individual self-control, however, is a matter of values, an ethos, a vision of what is right, expected, and desirable, plus an understanding of the probable consequences of not conforming—a culture, in short. It has to be built into police agencies and police behavior by training, constant emphasis, consistent action, and, as Pat Murphy understood, by leadership. Unhappily, not all police chiefs understand this.

In Los Angeles, Chief Daryl Gates was invited, by the mayor (whom he despised) and others, to accept responsibility for the King episode and what it implied about the culture of the department he had headed for fourteen years, and to resign. Chief Gates, who earlier in his career had promised himself never to be forced out of office, not very politely declined. However, the responsibility could only be his. The system in the LAPD, if not entirely his creation, was his responsibility—and he was its symbol. So persuaded was he of the LAPD's near perfection as a law-enforcement body (and, by implication, of his own near perfection because he so closely equated himself with the department), that when Amnesty International claimed to have evidence that the Rodney King event was not an aberration, but part of a pattern of beatings, torture, and other abuses, Gates simply dismissed the report as the ravings of "a bunch of knuckle-headed liberals who never see anything good."

Perhaps the saddest expression of the failure of leadership in Los Angeles, however, was the number of officers who stood around and watched their colleagues beat Mr. King; and even later, knowing that what had happened was wrong, who did nothing about it—even knowing that such inaction was wrong, too. Witnesses to an egregious event (Gates and the officers involved agreed it was that), which at least *may* have been a crime (the subsequent acquittal of the indicted officers can be construed as casting doubt on the point), they acted neither to stop it nor to apprehend the perpetrators—despite being on the scene and having a sworn duty to do both. They refrained from doing their duty, violated their sacred trust, we may surmise, mainly for the understandable but still unacceptable reason that the perpetrators were other police officers on whom they could not snitch. By betraying the public's trust and hope for temperate action and even-handed justice, these cops damaged the police institution, not only in Los Angeles, but everywhere.

Chief Gates seemed neither to understand this nor, despite his long experience, to recognize the fragility of the bond of trust that exists between the police and the policed. He therefore forfeited his right to head his agency. The mayor in Buffalo, New York, similarly, if less dramatically, missed the same point when he encouraged police officers *in uniform* to sell tickets to the public for a benefit on behalf of an indicted city official. In this case, fortunately, unlike that in Los Angeles, the Buffalo police chief saw his duty not in terms of personal loyalties but as a matter of larger institutional and public principles and forbade the activity.

CONTROLLING POLICE DISCRETION

Control of the police and its monopoly of force is vital to a free and civil society. Rules can help but cannot be relied on to do the job in the discretionary world of police work. Basically, as Gusfield stressed, it is a matter of "hearts and minds"—the undergirding concepts and tacit beliefs to which individuals are committed and on which their actions are grounded. The principal requirements of a police chief are not technical, but, as Pat Murphy would say, "spiritual." Management systems are important to operating any organization, but the key function of the executive, especially in a functionally decentralized system, is leadership: the will and ability to articulate a mission, an agenda, and a suitable set of legitimizing values for an enterprise, values to which others can commit their energies. The moral of the Rodney King story, then, is this: If there is a problem with the police in America, it is, as Tony Bouza says, more with the system and its leadership than with the rank and file.

Writing on this point in the *Law Enforcement News,* Klockars (1992) pointed out three primary ways in which police abuse of force is controlled. One is the criminal law (i.e., excessive force may constitute a crime). Another is civil liability (i.e., being sued and required to give compensation for causing injury); and the third is fear of scandal (by the officer and the agency). None of these, Klockars argues, is sufficient, chiefly because, being external and dealing only with actionable misconduct, they set too low a standard. Klockars illustrates the problem with an analogy:

> Suppose you were looking for a physician . . . and sought a recommendation from a friend who knew many area physicians. Your friend . . . suggest[s] Dr. Jones, with the following observations: Dr. Jones has never used his physician's powers criminally, he has never lost a malpractice suit, and has never been discovered to have engaged in scandalous behavior. Satisfied? Hardly. (p. 12)

Who would be? These standards obviously are insufficient. We have a right to expect more and to hope that police officers will expect more of themselves. Klockars believes that the route to obtaining more lies in police agencies devising policies on ways of working that minimize use of force *and* in development of conditions under which cops are willing and able to comply with them and to teach other officers how to comply. That this is difficult to do in practice, Gates (1992, Chapter 15) shows in a discussion of problems facing police officers in subduing violent parties, specifically via choke holds. Difficult or not, however, the need to minimize force remains.

Klockars perceives the self-protective "Cop's Code" as a primary impediment to such a program. Grounded, as the code is, in reaction to a punitively oriented command structure and a myriad of rules and regulations, if the code is to be neutralized, its conditions must at least be suspended. Klockars's answer to how to do that would invest heavily in development of a management and accountability structure and training of supervisors in using the system, on the one hand, and of officers, on the other hand, in improving their performance skills—in other words, substituting supervisory coaching for coercion, and training for punishment. Klockars's prescription, much like Bittner's and others', puts him squarely in a modern management mode a la Deming, Crosby, and the precepts of what now is commonly called "TQM" (total quality management): drive out the fear, improve the system, train, train, train, and, above all, articulate a mission and a value system to which the members of an organization can skillfully commit their energies.

In the specific context of policing, these modern management ideas have been embodied (not always knowingly) in the contemporary ideas of problem- and/or community-oriented policing that are being championed principally by a circle of academics: Herman Goldstein of the University of Wisconsin, J. Q. Wilson, and George Kelling at Harvard; by the Police Executive Research Forum (in its publications and by its leadership, especially its Executive Director, John Eck); and by such well-known police chiefs as Lee Brown in Atlanta, Houston, and New York (and a president of the IAPC) and David Couper in Madison, Wisconsin. Like other reform movements before it, this one too seeks to accomplish basic change in the frameworks and principles of police work and organization.

19

Changing the Culture of Policing

Goldstein's 1990 book, *Problem-Oriented Policing,* undoubtedly is the best single source on the subject. In it, he argues, like others from whom we have heard, that defining the role of policing as law enforcement is a mistaken idea. Problem-oriented policing is an explicit move against the traditional law-enforcement mission. It undertakes to redefine both the operational role of the police *and* the relationship between the police and the community. A more ambitious scheme for police reform than those of the past, Goldstein thinks—although, as we know from previous discussion, some earlier reform movements were pretty ambitious—problem-oriented policing is a distinctive perspective on policing. At once a concept, a theory, a philosophy, and a plan for policing, its principal tenets, according to Goldstein (p. 179), are these:

- policing consists of dealing with a wide range of quite different problems, not just with crime
- these problems are interrelated, and the priority given them must be reassessed rather than ranked in traditional ways
- each problem requires a different response, not a generic response that is applied to all problems
- use of the criminal law is but one means of responding to a problem, it is not the only means
- police can accomplish much in working to prevent problems rather than simply responding efficiently to an endless number of incidents that are merely the manifestations of problems
- developing an effective response to a problem requires prior analysis rather than simply invoking traditional practices
- the capacity of the police is extremely limited, despite the impression of omnipotence that the police cultivate and others believe
- the police role is more akin to that of facilitators, enabling and encouraging the community to maintain its norms governing behavior, rather than an agency that assumes total responsibility for doing so

COMMUNITY-ORIENTED POLICING

Goldstein distinguishes between but recognizes a connection between problem-oriented policing (POP) and community-oriented policing (COP), and between each of them and private-sector management-improvement ideas such as Deming's (Walton, 1986). POP-COP can, however, be seen as a particular version of the managerial ethos that goes under the contemporary banner of TQM. Indeed, Couper's (Couper & Lobitz, 1991b) book on quality policing (a term Goldstein also uses) makes the point explicit.

Problem-Oriented Policing, Community-Oriented Policing, and Total Quality Management

The fact is that the TQM movement is by no means confined to the private sector. The New York State Governor's Award for management excellence, the Excelsior Award, which is modeled, with modifications, on the Malcolm Baldrige National Quality Award, is given to public sector and educational organizations, as well as to private sector ones. As a matter of fact, the first public-sector winner of the Excelsior Award (in 1992) was the New York State Police.[1]

POP-COP is thus of a piece with a modern managerial current, the essential precepts of which correspond closely with the ones advanced by Goldstein:

- Customer orientation and an idea of production systems as supplier-customer chains
- Belief in the unacceptability of error and in continuous improvement
- Proactive problem-seeking, with problems viewed as opportunities for improvement
- Concentration on work-process control and improvement
- Emphasis on planning and measurement
- Long-term perspective on development
- Stress on human resources excellence, training, development, and empowerment
- Emphasis on lateral relations not hierarchy, cross-functional integration, and teams as problem-solving units
- Orientation toward management of internal and external relationships via collaboration or partnering

The linkage between POP-COP and TQM, and its plausibility as a premise for reform of policing in American, warrants further careful reflection, beginning with Goldstein's tripartite thesis, which runs as follows:

First, the impersonal apolitical Taylorist professional model of Vollmer, O. W. Wilson, and others with its emphasis on centralized control, close supervision, high standards of selection and training, narrow definitions of function and responsibility, operational efficiency, and lawful action, has been subject to criticism since the 1960s at least.

Second, this criticism has been informed by research findings on the actual practices of police on the street: their informal handling of incidents rather than executing standard operating procedures (SOPs); the conditioning of police behavior by a variety of circumstantial influences quite apart from (although not necessarily in violation of) legal mandates; the use of arrest not only as a step in the criminal justice system (CJS) but also as a means of accomplishing a range of objectives additional to prosecuting miscreants (harassment, investigation, safekeeping, punishment, etc.); elaboration by street cops of a repertoire of informal techniques outside the CJS to handle situations; the omnipresence of discretionary decision making by cops on the street; by reports from a set of national studies (among them, the 1967 President's Commission on Law Enforcement and Administration of Justice, and the 1973 National Advisory Commission on Criminal Justice Standards and Goals) that, while implicitly sustaining a professional model of police work, raised new questions about functions, accountability, and community relations; and by certain experiments in police work, such as the Kansas City Preventive Patrol study (Kelling, Pate, Dieckman, & Brown, 1974), all of which, Goldstein suggests, seemed to indicate

> that the police erred in doggedly investing so much of police resources in a limited number of practices, based in retrospect, on some rather naive and simplistic concepts of the police. . . . [and that] improvements in policing must be based on a fuller recognition of the complexity of the police task. (p. 13)

Third, nevertheless, the field of policing remains (a) "preoccupied with management, internal procedures, and efficiency" at the expense of an interest in dealing effectively with problems; (b) reactively oriented to calls from citizens rather than proactively acting on its own initiative to "prevent or reduce community problems"; (c) inattentive to the community as a resource for understanding and preventing problems from becoming the usual business of the police; (d) unable to make effective use of the "time and talents" of the rank and file; or (e) unwilling or unable to frame policies and organizations that can "accommodate and support change."

Problem-Oriented Policing, Community-Oriented Policing, and the Nature of Police Work

As evidence of the indifference of the field of policing to what Goldstein calls the "substantive" tasks of policing—that is, to the essential, primary, basic ones—he notes that most of the leading textbooks in the field, the professional and academic journals, the topics discussed at professional meetings, college courses, and the ways chiefs actually spend their time heavily stress the merely procedural exercises of police work and ways to make it more efficient (Mayo, 1985).

Goldstein accepts that running a police department is demanding and time-binding. Doing it efficiently therefore is important, obviously. In addition, coming to grips with the large, difficult, and ambiguous substantive aspects of police work is daunting and risky. Just where and how the police legitimately relate to community problems often is neither clear nor well-agreed on. Hence, the police go on seeking operational efficiencies mainly in reacting to floods of incidents, the volume of which has benefited from motorized patrols, hugely augmented communications capabilities, the ubiquitous telephone (and 911), and professional pride in high response rates and low response times. As Goldstein says: "In the vast majority of police departments, the telephone, more than any policy decision by the community or by management, [dictates] how police resources will be used" (p. 20). Chief Daryl Gates, who, incidentally, claims that COP was invented by the LAPD, also remarks on the often frenetic incident-driven quality of police work.

"A community," Goldstein however argues, "must police itself. The police can, at best, only assist in that task" (p. 21). Reactive, procedurally preoccupied, professional approaches to policing as law enforcement, he maintains, estrange the police from the community, quite as Wilson and Kelling argued in their widely cited 1982 "Broken Windows" article. POP-COP's goal is to change this reactively impersonal incident-driven form of policing.

POLICE AND THE MAINTENANCE OF COMMUNITY ORDER

Arguing that physical deterioration and/or disorderly behavior in neighborhoods tends to spread and ultimately to prompt a collapse of public order and crime, Wilson and Kelling's (1982) paper, in a social context of growing popular anxiety about crime, public safety, and the degraded ambience of American cities, stimulated popular interest in the role of the police in managing public order as distinct from crime per se. Community policing, the idea of enlisting the citizenry in a partnership with the police to improve the quality of life in a locale, was one response to this interest.

Neither COP nor POP has standard definitions at this point; nor do they have an altogether common repertoire of practices. Implementation of POP-COP sometimes amounts to little more than increasing the use of foot patrols in a neighborhood. However, Goldstein thinks that two general patterns of practice have emerged from among the varied activities represented as either POP or COP. One is broad, ambitious, and amorphous. Goldstein refers to it as a popular movement that seeks to develop sweepingly new relationships between the police and the community, to improve the quality of those relationships, and to encourage collaboration in solving community problems.

The other approach to COP orients more toward particular issues or problems. In this much more limited community engagement (e.g., a neighborhood crime watch program), the citizenry is enlisted in an effort to deal with a specific matter of interest to both (i.e., burglary). Also the community in question may simply be defined as those affected by the problem.

Clearly the first of these two forms of policing poses the greater challenges and, as Goldstein points out, raises many complex issues about what is to be done and where, who is to do what, how and when. Simply defining a "community" may itself prove difficult, as may determining the conditions necessary to its effective engagement in its own policing. Also there are inevitable questions about containing the scope of police power and authority in the amorphous processes of "problem solving." Moreover, unlike the ad hoc community coalitions formed in the limited-scope version of POP-COP, its more expansive counterpart intends to forge a permanent partnership between the police and the community. Its goal is not so much to solve particular problems as it is to change relationships between the police and the community.

Goldstein himself is dubious about the prospects for this grand design, which he finds "reminiscent of past police reforms." Anyway, he fears it will continue to foster a preoccupation with means over ends. From Goldstein's perspective, then, it is better to concentrate on substantive problems—the work to be done and its results—rather than on "organizational and institutional arrangements for providing police services" (p. 26). Hence, given what he perceives to be the state of policing today, he suspects that productive engagements between the police and the community are likely to be easiest if officers are simply assigned to areas long enough to reach an understanding of the problems that concern the residents of a community (in the language of TQM, to reach an understanding of the "customer's requirements"); to build a capability (develop "databases") for analyzing community problems; to comprehend when more community involvement can helpfully affect a problem; and then work with specific relevant parties to eliminate or reduce the problem, to improve the quality of life in the area.

In the process, Goldstein's program emphasizes making the best use of "the men and women who provide police services to the public" (p. 27): To inform their discretion, develop their craft skills, and exploit to the fullest their knowledge of substantive community problems and what works in handling them—to encourage and reward them for thinking and being creative in their work.

PROBLEM-ORIENTED POLICING RATHER THAN COMMUNITY-ORIENTED POLICING?

From the foregoing discussion, one can easily discern Goldstein's reasons for leaning more toward POP than toward COP. He simply thinks that it is more feasible and has fewer down-side risks. Goldstein's agenda, albeit in the framework of a limited version of POP, is not, however, simply to tinker with police operations. He wants to accomplish major changes in the craft of policing: the general practices, orientations, and values of the police—in other words, he wants a change in the culture of policing. Cognizant of the fact that the existing police "subculture," as he calls it, is resistive to change, Goldstein imagines a process of transformation that is likely to be gradual, incremental, and opportunistic, rather than formally and systematically planned according to some grand design. However, change can be nonetheless purposeful, Goldstein thinks, if it is guided by "a coherent vision of the ideal arrangements for providing police services" (p. 31). Goldstein's vision (his version of Deming's "14 Points," so to speak) for the police in America is composed of what he believes to be the basic defining rudiments of POP.

1. Heretofore, as we have heard, the basic *work unit* of policing has been the isolated "incident" (e.g., a specific occurrence of car theft), toward the handling of which the professional model applied primarily efficiency standards, without encouraging exploration of factors ("root causes" in TQM-speak) that may have led to the incident.

2. POP now seeks a move beyond the incident by requiring police officers to look for *relationships* between incidents (e.g., commonalities of actors, behaviors, places, circumstances) that can be seen as defining *classes* of incidents (or the problems, which are the basic objects of POP), and to take a more analytic attitude toward finding causes of these problems.

3. Groupings of frequently recurring incidents, thus, define the substantive problems that constitute the objects or units of police work, and solutions to these problems constitute the *products* of that work.

4. Problems may be defined in different ways, of course (e.g., as troublesome behavior or as troublesome places), and at different levels (e.g., a specific park or a whole city), but they always are to be defined in terms of the *concerns of the people affected by them* (the customers, clients, or constituencies for police services), which means that the police must have means of knowing, understanding, and considering these concerns.

5. The essential standard for evaluating the quality of policing is its effectiveness in actually meeting the requirements of the customer by *resolving* substantive problems, not its procedural efficiency. (On page 36 of his 1990 book, Goldstein describes an illustrative effectiveness scale developed by Eck and Spelman of PERF, which recognizes five levels of impact on a problem by a police intervention: [a] total elimination, [b] reducing the number of incidents, [c] reducing the seriousness of the incidents, [d] designing better methods for handling incidents, and [e] removing the problem from police jurisdiction.) However, focusing on the substantive, community problems that the police must handle is a much more radical step than it initially appears to be, for it requires the police to go beyond taking satisfaction in the smooth operation of their organization; it requires that they extend their concern to dealing effectively with the problems that justify creating a police agency in the first instance (p. 35).

6. To Goldstein, this suggests a characterization of the police role as one of "managing deviance" (although why and how it is to be construed so is unclear, and, in fact, the central definitional question of what constitutes the business of the police in the POP-COP context remains vague and itself problematic).

7. Effective problem solving requires careful and systematic inquiry (data gathering, research, analysis, and dissemination), which police agencies must learn to value, to use, and to develop the skills for doing, both for problem definition and to translate requirements for solutions into specifications for police actions or processes.

8. Effective problem solving also requires the development of historical records and usable databases regarding appropriately coded problems and not simply generically labeled phenomena (e.g., those of the criminal code such as robbery, burglary, etc.), which may mask important distinctions among problems that are necessary to effective solution finding.

9. Critical assessment of the "nature of the police concern" with a particular problem (e.g., prostitution) must go beyond the idea that it is against the law toward an evaluation of the community interests in it (who is affected and how), an evaluation that should be factual and quantitative, so that priorities for action can be stated.

10. Problems must be viewed in relation to an agency's current response to them, which requires this response to be documented (difficult as that may be with officers on the street) and critiqued against the requirements for an effective solution.

11. Effective responses to particular problems will be imaginative and microsurgically tailor-made rather than standardized, which necessitates "breaking out of the mold of looking only within the criminal justice system for solutions" (p. 44).

12. Problem solving requires a proactive police stance—"more assertive" decision making—in dealing with developing problems, in advising the community on possibilities for handling its concerns, and in forming partnerships with other public agencies on behalf of community interests. (Goldstein is not unaware that an advocacy role for the police has its dangers. The question, obviously, is how to set limits, avoid abuse, and ensure moderation in choosing. He does not, however, give specific answers to the question. Instead, he talks, in effect, about the risk of greater police initiative being necessary to achieve effective management of community problems. Presumably, the inculcation of values, the training, and the kinds of team-based policing envisaged by the quality-management strategies we discuss at greater length subsequently can serve to build conditions in the police agency that foster self-regulation.)

13. POP requires risk-taking and accountability in actions, which once again raises the question of potential abuse of discretion, as Goldstein knows, but thinks, perhaps a bit Pollyannaishly, will somehow be okay in the high-accountability environment of POP.

14. Effectiveness requires evaluation of implemented solutions, which requires not only suitable skills within police agencies but also openness to outside specialists, such as academics, and partnerships with funding agencies.

NOTE

1. In January, 1993, the International Association of Chiefs of Police formally announced its own "Quality in Law Enforcement Award Program" (*Police Chief,* January 1993, p. 13). The Seavey Award, as it will be called in honor of the IACP's first president, Webber Seavey of Omaha, Nebraska, is modeled on the Baldrige National Quality Award. It was developed by the IACP in association with the Motorola Corporation, a winner of one of the first Baldrige Awards in 1988 (and of the first New York Excelsior Awards in 1992). Annual world-wide competitions will be held for three awards designed to allow even the smallest agencies to compete.

The stated objectives for the Quality in Law Enforcement Award are to 1) improve the quality of local law enforcement; 2) enhance police services; 3) strengthen community relations; 4) improve the use of departmental resources, such as, productivity; and 5) develop innovative means of intra- and inter-agency cooperation. For Motorola's part, developing the Seavey Award was a "model" for public-private partnering. The IACP, meanwhile, wishes to help ". . . literally redefine the concept of law enforcement" (p. 13).

20

Leadership in the New Paradigm of Problem-Oriented Policing

Goldstein (and most others in the POP-COP movement) put great trust in leadership as the ultimate means and guarantor of ethically effective policing. In the Selznickian fashion, leaders are expected to articulate a sense of purpose for their organizations and with it a set of guiding values to which the organization's members can subscribe and which, as they are institutionalized, then will shape their individual decisions.

Changing the ideas of the police always is hard to do, as in fact it is with any cohesive group. To be influential, a leader requires a means of deploying ideas and principles throughout her or his organization to the end that the organization works as a unitary system and not a collection of distinct functional (and cultural) enclaves. Deployment, in turn, requires communication, incentives, removal of barriers to rank-and-file involvement in management, and appropriate working role models.

The organizational deployment of a coherent community- and problem-oriented operating philosophy necessarily and quickly confronts a problem of supervision: getting middle managers and first-line supervisors to commit to the philosophy. Goldstein, in fact, thinks it may be easier to change the rank and file than the first line (sergeants, lieutenants). The simplified mechanistic routinization of customary police operations makes supervisory jobs easier than they may seem to be in the more dynamic, ambiguously organic framework of POP-COP, with all its emphasis on street-cop initiative. As Goldstein observes, not much in the training or experience of sergeants readies them for work in the weakened-authority POP-COP mode. It is understandably threatening to them, and they resist its implementation.

Goldstein thinks that training, role-modeling, support, and leadership are important to converting supervisors to the new paradigm, but in the end, conversion surely will depend on the workings of the police department's reward system: who gets promoted and on what criteria. This sends messages about the organization's seriousness of purpose—its readiness to put its money where its mouth is, and it gradually populates the ranks of supervision with converts to the new system, thereby deploying the message and helping to make it a natural way of life.

An axiom of POP-COP is decentralization:

> Taken aback by the degree of alienation, and forced to reflect on the extent to which police work depends on a positive, continuing relationship with the community and on an accumulation of knowledge about the community, police agencies executed a dramatic about face in their attitudes about centralization. It was reflected in the move to establish new precincts, ministations, and storefront offices. It led eventually to the more advanced forms of community policing in which the most important element is usually the permanent assignment of an officer to a neighborhood. (Goldstein, 1990, p. 160)

The old efficiency- and control-obsessed model of policing inevitably drove hierarchy, rules, and SOPs, in essential denial of the situational and discretionary nature of policing, while distancing the (usually motorized) patrol officer from the citizenry. Moreover, it undervalued the knowledge of community characteristics and problems held by police officers and discouraged them from deepening and acting on their knowledge.

Thus the fundamental problem with the so-called traditional twentieth-century professional law-enforcement model of policing, which POP-COP hopes to replace, is that it ended up (unintentionally, of course) being effectively antirational. What policing, therefore, needs is, yes, modernization. It needs to become a fact-based, planned operation, designed to find and solve community problems. Also, cops need to develop a whole new set of attitudes and skills in areas such as interpersonal relations and research and analysis, which have not been customarily thought of as real police work, and which, as Goldstein comments, in the prevailing police culture may not even be seen as working but as "goofing off."

Making these kinds of changes, Goldstein believes, takes "unique chiefs and their immediate subordinates to assume this broadened leadership role" (1990, p. 155). It is hard to miss in this rhetoric an iconic image of the police chief as hero. The leadership role is important, as we, too, have insisted, but if it requires truly unique individuals to play it, then, taking into account that there are thousands of police departments, there is not much chance of widespread change occurring, as, in reality, so far there has not been.

LINKING WITH THE QUALITY MOVEMENT

POP-COP is part of a worldwide pattern of institutional and organizational change that has spanned the past 50 or so years. Its current manifestation as quality management expresses a progressive development in managerial ideology (and practice), rooted in ideas that emerged in the 1920s and 1930s, were articulated by Shewhart and Deming before World War II, and have been systematically applied in Japan since the 1950s.

In the *Law Enforcement News* of May 15, 1992, Angelo Pisani questioned whether a plan to add up to 6000 additional police in New York City, to implement community policing, is the wisest use of public funds. He noted, for instance, that crime rose in Houston after COP was introduced. Nevertheless, Pisani fatalistically observed that COP is "part of a reform movement that is sweeping the nation" (p. 13). Indeed it is: in Aurora, Colorado; Boston; Portland, Oregon; San Francisco; Tulsa, Oklahoma; New York City; Madison, Wisconsin; Lansing, Michigan; Baltimore; Houston (at least until recently); and (maybe) Los Angeles (see *Time* magazine, April 1, 1991).

In the Madison, Wisconsin, police chief's preface to his book, *Quality Policing* (1991b), David Couper and his wife, Sabine Lobitz (a sergeant in the Wisconsin Capitol police), quote Detective Alix Olson of the Madison Police Department's Experimental Police District, who observed that "many police departments nationwide are . . . implementing problem-oriented policing" (p. v). Couper and Lobitz then went on to describe Madison's ambitious and determined efforts in this direction. Doing so, they are explicit about the connection between the ideas of POP-COP and the broader worldwide managerial ethos of TQM, arguing, for instance, that "the problems that are endemic in the business world are also endemic in police service" (p. 4): a short-term orientation, shallow thinking, and quick-fix responses. The solutions to these problems in police departments can be expected to take operational forms that mirror the particulars of police work but, at the same time, they will presumably express a more universal conceptual and ideological foundation not at all specific to policing.

Couper and Lobitz define the goal of quality policing as "[achieving] long-term, total citizen-customer satisfaction as defined by the customer" (p. 13). Clearly, this could equally well be the goal of AT&T, Dunlop Tire, Chevrolet, Fisher-Price Toys, or Joe's Shoe Repair. The hyphenated *citizen-*customer in Couper and Lobitz's goal statement is the only thing that suggests anything faintly different about the Madison Police Department and Joe's Shoe Repair.

TOTAL QUALITY MANAGEMENT
AND THE POLICE

Couper and Lobitz's vision of quality policing puts heavy emphasis on leadership and leader roles, as do most TQM advocates. They speak of a reform style of leadership, however, which is nonauthoritarian, problem-oriented, and open to new ideas from both inside and outside the police organization. Couper and Lobitz see hierarchy as a basic problem of contemporary police organization. They perceive the traditional steep command-and-control rank structure and the idea of managers as the experts who run the department to be counterproductive as well as unrealistic.

As a replacement, they envisage a decentralized system of problem-solving teams trained and empowered to make and implement their own decisions under guidance chiefly from their commitment to the principles of quality policing, to which principles they are accountable. As for the customary role of the "police as enforcer," that was left behind in the 1970s, in favor of an idea of the "police as peacekeeper," in Madison at any rate. Madison's early moves toward quality policing ran into problems with a union reluctant about going along in the new direction of TQM. Disputes, grievances, and even litigation were frequent. This has abated with time and with increased union involvement in quality programs.

Couper and Lobitz report on an impressive array of programs and other organizational initiatives to install quality policing that began in Madison in the early 1980s, when Couper, after returning from an apparently restorative sabbatical, "decided," he said, "to take on some of the department's internal problems." By 1985, Madison's mayor had initiated a separate citywide quality and productivity effort oriented around "Deming methods" that complemented and supported the police department's. The mayor's interest in quality themes, Couper and Lobitz believe, was "a critical factor in the success of the police department" (p. 23).

Couper and Lobitz describe a large number of activities and programs by which, since the mid-1960s, the Madison department sought to move in the "new direction" and implement quality policing. A sense of their scope, content, and tone can be seen from the following simple listing:

- Establishment of police officers' advisory councils
- Formation of a committee on the future of the department
- Forging of links with the city's quality/productivity efforts
- Attending Deming seminars
- Employing outside consultants
- Training team leaders and process facilitators
- Developing a department mission statement, emphasizing community orientation, problem-solving policing, attention to employees and quality of the workplace
- Running a variety of other training activities, and doing lots of training
- Forming cross-functional management teams
- Using trained process facilitators in team meetings

- Instituting neighborhood patrol bureaus ("to get closer to the people we serve")
- Instituting foot patrols
- Maintaining "beat integrity"
- Opening neighborhood "cop shops"
- Training and using cops as community organizers and problem solvers, helping to improve quality of life in neighborhoods
- Establishing an experimental police district to test ideas
- Involving the police union in quality initiatives
- Doing "internal customer" surveys
- Conducting regular "external customer" (citizen) surveys
- Using survey data for system improvement, changing management styles, improving communications, and so forth
- Formulating a statement on "Principles of Quality Leadership" emphasizing active, system-changing leadership
- Conducting seminars on quality leadership
- Doing continuous team-building
- Developing "quality champions" (who sign quality leadership commitments)
- Ensuring active chief involvement in programs
- Establishing an office of quality coordinator (as a champion for quality, a teacher, and a coach)
- Forming a departmental quality leadership council
- Using an outside coach (a person from the city's Community Services Bureau) and internal mentoring
- Developing data and statistical analyses to find the "special causes" of problems
- Formation of a quality leadership academy
- A lot of "Management by Wandering About" by the chief (who is usually in uniform)

Quality policing in Madison is clearly a top-down affair, but with a lot of bottom-up feedback. Its idea of *leader* (a term it prefers to *manager* because it seems more "active") is a service provider to subordinates, who are viewed as the "customers" of these leaders and so are to be satisfied by them. Hence, it is necessary for manager-leaders to get feedback from these subordinates about how well their requirements are being met— ergo, internal customer surveys.

WHITHER HEARTS AND MINDS?

The Madison police department took a major step toward institution-alization of its new TQM philosophy via a chief-driven process of awarding promotions to officers "who were peer group leaders and who wished to adopt the Quality Leadership style," who were flexible, and who had strong interpersonal and facilitative skills (Couper & Lobitz, 1991b, p. 63). Over time, the result of such a reoriented reward system would be a new and different cadre of leaders for the organization's transformation (not all of whom would have been promoted under the old regime). Moreover, visibly tuning an organization's reward system is a compelling way of communicating the values according to which it intends to operate.

There is very little, however, about ethics or morality in the Madison Police Department's statement of the "Principles of Quality Leadership" or in the chief's "vision" of what he is after:

> The department is a dynamic organization devoted to improvement, excellence, maintaining customer satisfaction, and operating on the principles of Quality Leadership. Key characteristics: teamwork, data-based decision-making, part of the community, neighborhood services, networking-participative, systems oriented, creative, and improving. (p. 69)

Thus Chief Couper's vision statement is inexplicit on the moral dimension of the hearts-and-minds issue. Both it and the principles of quality leadership to which it refers are relatively more occupied with the mechanics of operations. It may be argued, however, that in order to change an organization's culture, the ways in which it operates must change—and the ways in which a police department operates are what counts. Arguably, too, Madison's concentration on knowing and satisfying the requirements of its citizen-customers inevitably implies a fundamental respect and concern for its customers' welfare *and* an active departmental orientation toward its enhancement.

Couper and Lobitz's manager-leader is a heroic figure. Among other things, he or she "must have the courage to break with tradition, even to the point of exile among . . . peers" (p. 91). If sometimes overdone, this kind of rhetoric is not altogether out of place. Chief Daryl Gates to the contrary notwithstanding, this POP-COP/TQM stuff is a very big step in policing. It seeks to change police roles *and* the bases for their legitimation. It reverses the formal abstract *legal* basis of authority that has dominated policing during the twentieth century in favor of a situated variety (which, however, is no less rational in purpose). It seeks major structural change in police organizations: from centralized mechanistic performance-oriented to decentralized organic problem-solving systems; from external integration by an impersonal command-and-control structure to internal integration around a common purpose. This also demands a compatible redefinition of police work itself as discretionary service delivery rather than standardized law enforcement.

Criticism of POP-COP has come in a variety of forms, from a variety of quarters, some of it practical (e.g., costs), some of it principled. In Geller's (1985) anthology, Kerstetter addressed the question of who does and who should discipline the police, mainly with reference to use of *non*deadly force. He dealt with a number of issues, including administrative accountability and various ways of ensuring it. In the process, he placed his emphasis on "creating a balanced system that defers substantially to police expertise" and on "customary" (as distinct from specifically legal) bases for deciding the legitimacy of police roles and actions. The idea that law and professional expertise are the primary foundations of legitimacy, Kerstetter insisted, is wrong. The police officer, he argued, whether acting as a person or a legal officer, is expected to deal with situations that violate customs and morality more than law and relies primarily on informal control in doing it. Order maintenance, therefore, best describes the officer's role, and civilian monitors are its best judges.

In rebuttal of Kerstetter's thesis, Wesley A. Carrol ("Wes") Pomeroy, a former police chief in Berkeley, California, linked Kerstetter's arguments directly with Wilson and Kelling's, which he interpreted as implying that "a democracy can tolerate extralegal or even illegal behavior by its police" (1985, p. 183). In a general critique of "situationalist" models of police work (e.g., Bittner's or Goldstein's), Pomeroy maintained that the police are creatures and instruments of *law* and must be thus constrained.

Also in rebuttal of Kerstetter, Amitai Schwartz (1985), of the American Civil Liberties Union, declared that policing is "the public's business" (p. 187) and that its control is not an internal matter—internal to the police, that is. External control is required to limit police discretion because, for one good reason, "police investigation has rarely worked to protect constitutional rights" (p. 187).

Finally, George Napper (1985), a police commissioner in Atlanta, replies to Kerstetter and his question, "Who should discipline the police?" by saying the answer is straightforward: "I do!" It is the *chief,* working with the citizenry, Napper insists, who is accountable for police behavior and so must be their disciplinarian.

There may be many reasons in addition to principle why an individual police chief is attracted to the POP-COP/TQM enthusiasm, including simply because it is the "in" thing among progressive modern managers. Its stress on teamwork, common purposes, joint problem solving, and whatnot, may, however, seem to imply another virtue: depoliticization of policing—a way out of the political arena, modernization without the pain.

In fact, however, POP-COP/TQM is no less rationalist than its traditional alternative. Like any good rationalists (or Taylorists, for that matter), Couper and Lobitz describe quality policing as "a process of making deliberate, knowing choices" (p. 58), and of planning for continuous improvement (p. 59). Also, remember that Bittner still wants to put policing on a "fully reasoned basis." Furthermore, Goldstein's POP is no moral cru- sade, but an argument for good sense, technical proficiency, and data-based management.

21

Modern Police Roles

Shifting from Bittner's traditional professional model of policing to POP has the effect of increasing the complexity of police work. It leaves behind any idea of police work as routine and the police officer as a rote performer of fixed practices. Instead, it conceives of police work as a matter of ad hoc decision making on how best to handle particular cases of deviance (or of whatever else needs to be done), while trying to identify and prevent the reasons why those things happen. This is a very big change in concept, which requires new principles, tools, and structures to suit the new way of thinking and working—tools and structures of the kind described by Couper and Lobitz.

At the same time, the POP-COP phenomenon mirrors developments in the world of management generally. Since the late nineteenth century, when a conception of organizations as complex production systems emerged, patterns of orientation toward their management have appeared and changed, as attention shifted to and from different aspects of production processes and prompted thought about how best to handle their complexities.

Early management theorists, for instance, concentrated on the input aspects of production. Seeking to economize on resources, they focused on the *efficiency* of operating systems and ways to maximize it. Interest subsequently gravitated to the output from the production system and its conformity to specifications: in other words, to *product quality,* and its control, mainly by inspection. Products that passed quality control were accepted while others became rework or scrap. An emphasis on the *processes* by which products were produced came later. With it came efforts to control the variability of those processes and to improve their capability in order to ensure that outputs would consistently conform to the requirements specified for them and would thereby eliminate scrap and rework.

Finally, as a foundation for planning, monitoring, and guiding performance, *TQM* represents an effort to take and act on an integrative view of the entire production system (from its suppliers through to its customers or beneficiaries), with special attention to the human and nonhuman resources

142

required for a system to operate, and to the circumstances of its environment. Most of the particular operational features of TQM follow from its heavily context-based emphasis on the production process (Ciampa, 1991, may be consulted for a solid general review of TQM and its methodologies). TQM, which Joiner (1985) aptly calls "fourth-generation management," if not revolutionary, is certainly a major progressive development in management thinking and practice, which carries important implications for changing organizational cultures.

Thinking about policing as a production system is comparatively new. As we saw in Part I, earlier phases of police modernization largely held to an input focus and preoccupied itself with using police resources efficiently in law enforcement. The current POP-COP/ TQM enthusiasm denotes a significant shift in police thinking toward a process orientation and the development of effective ways of defining, doing, and evaluating police work. The police industry seems to have skipped an intermediate product-oriented stage of development.

QUALITY MANAGEMENT AS CULTURE CHANGE

TQM aims at the development and management of culture.[1] The founding technical logic of its philosophy is in the principle of variation, the idea that organizational energy needs to be directed to the identification and elimination of sources of error in a production process (i.e., toward problems), and to the development of robust methods that yield consistent performance. TQM, however, is also a humanistic philosophy based on a logic of cooperative or participative management. Thus TQM represents a coming together of scientific and humanistic conviction in the second half of the twentieth century.

TQM advocates, whether gurus or tyros, do not often link their ideas with the academic literature on management. However, it is easy to divine congruencies between TQM and three separate streams of management thought: the so-called classical and scientific management school, human relations in management, and general systems theory. Taylor (1947) himself described scientific management as a "mental revolution." What was dressed out in the forms of a management technology—flow charts, time study, forward planning, and so on—soon became a state of mind and a search for the one best way to do a task.

Neither scientific management nor TQM were discrete inventions. They were and are more exactly the systematic integration of ideas and techniques (most of them entirely familiar) into a normative theory of management— a theory, moreover, that obviously has spread far beyond the shop floor.

Taylor's analytic but mechanistic approach, as we have seen, promoted an external strategy of management oriented toward directing and controlling employees in their work. His approach to personnel management was heavily co-optative (better pay and simpler work). The integrative emphases of TQM, however, imply a more active cooperative partnership for effective operation among an organization's numerous constituencies—ideas that were emphasized in the 1930s by Mary Parker Follet (see Metcalf & Urwick, 1942) and Chester Barnard (1938).

Follet, in fact, advanced a view of organization as a process of continuous problem solving. At the same time, beginning generally with the work of Mayo and his associates at Western Electric's Hawthorne plant (Roethlisberger & Dickson, 1939), attention focused on the motivations and attitudes of individual workers and their informal relationships with one another in the factory as important determinants in the performance of work. These same sentiments are echoed by TQM's operational emphasis on teams, teamwork, and self-managing work groups—both as means of ensuring effective operations and as vehicles for the problem solving essential for continuous improvement.

The antithesis of "human relations in industry" to the mechanistic Taylorist thesis of scientific management was bridged in the 1960s and 1970s by a so-called sociotechnical school that emphasized a systemic view of organization. This theory of organization-as-system simply made interdependence its cornerstone. An organization and its performance, in short, result from a complex interplay of factors internal and external to it: technologies, human motivations, and environmental forces.

There is no Taylorist "one best way" to do a task; different ways may be equally effective, depending on the context. By the same token, what works in one place or time may not work in another, if conditions are different. Obviously, then, it is essential to effective management that problem solving be context based. This open-system ethos is apparent in the rhetoric of TQM, wherein organizing is imagined as a complex and ongoing process, the structuring and management of which requires flexibility and constant adjustment to changing circumstances.

LEADERSHIP AGAIN

The leadership theme so prominent in writings on TQM, and institutionalized by its inclusion among the evaluation categories of the Baldrige and Excelsior awards, reflects a sturdy Western cultural tradition of top-down management. TQM itself usually is described as a "top-down" improvement strategy, the success of which heavily depends on the vision, commitment, and energy of organizations' chief executives. However, this vertical emphasis has as much or more to do with the problematics of implementing planned change as it has with the fundamentals of quality processes, per se.

Once TQM operating systems are firmly in place, as they have been for 40 years in many Japanese companies, the high-profile visionary role of top management as champion of quality is likely to move in the lower-key direction of maintaining the culture of quality and encouraging its incremental enhancement, with succeeding managers building incrementally on the accomplishments of their predecessors (Fukuda, 1983). Indeed, in a mature TQM (or POP-COP) environment, the role of management is likely to become somewhat defensive. Organic, problem-oriented environments are yeasty places characterized by high levels of uncertainty, ad hoc decision making, and risk. They lack the attractive tranquility of standardized, mechanistic systems. Simply maintaining an organization as an organic, problem-solving system, therefore, becomes an active responsibility of its senior management.

TQM (or POP-COP) in most organizations today, however, is a large aspiration for changing cultures that remains much more an aspiration than it is a reality. The difficulties of initiating, sustaining, and legitimizing large undertakings, such as the conversion of police agencies to problem-solving systems, are well known. Transformational leadership probably is critical to overcoming them, surely in the early phases of the process. Framing visions of an achievable organizational future, articulating the principles and values according to which decisions can be made and evaluated and actions legitimized on the way to that future, and acting to develop programs and systems that translate the new ideology into everyday practices are responsibilities of top managers—and in police departments, of police chiefs. It is furthermore a political responsibility.

A comparative advantage of police chiefs, as public authorities, rests not in their control of material resources with which to satisfy the needs and wants of citizens and police officers, but, perhaps more importantly, in their control of symbols of expertise and legitimacy, channels of communication by which to disseminate these in society, and the societal structures of decision making. Politics, then, as we have explained, is a normative contest: a struggle for hearts and minds.

This, we would repeat, is the spiritual dimension of Murphy's job description for a police chief. Of course, management is important to operating any organization, but the essential function of the principal executive is leadership: the will and the ability to articulate a mission, an agenda, and a set of legitimizing values for an enterprise, and to develop operational means for their expression and to which others can commit their energies (Selznick, 1957). So, where are you, Masked Person?

NOTE

1. In what follows here, we have relied heavily on an unpublished paper entitled "The Roots of Total Quality Management" by Judy Shippengrover (1992), Department of Educational Administration, State University of New York at Buffalo.

References

Banton, M. (1964). *The Policeman in the Community*. New York: Basic Books.

Barnard, C. (1938). *The Functions of the Executive*. Cambridge, MA: Harvard University Press.

Bayley, D. H. (1979). Police function, structure, and control in Western Europe and North America: Comparative and historical studies. In N. Morris & M. Tonry (Eds.), *Crime and Justice: An Annual Review of Research* (Vol. 1, pp. 109-143). Chicago: University of Chicago Press.

Bell, D. J. (1981). Collective bargaining: Perspective for the 1980s. *Journal of Police Science and Administration, 9,* 296-305.

Berman, J. S. (1987). *Police Administration and Progressive Reform: Theodore Roosevelt as Police Commissioner of New York*. New York: Greenwood Press.

Biddle, B. J. (1979). *Role Theory*. New York: Academic Press.

Bittner, E. (1970). *The Functions of the Police in Modern Society*. Washington, DC: U.S. Government Printing Office.

Bittner, E. (1990). *Aspects of Police Work*. Boston: Northeastern University Press.

Black, D. (1980). *The Manners and Customs of the Police*. New York: Academic Press.

Bordua, D. J., & Reiss, A. J., Jr. (1966). Command, control, and charisma. *American Journal of Sociology, 72,* 68-76.

Bouza, A. V. (1978). *Police Administration, Organization and Performance*. New York: Pergamon.

Bouza, A. V. (1985). Police unions: Paper tigers or roaring lions? In W. A. Geller (Ed.), *Police Leadership in America* (pp. 241-280). New York: Praeger.

Bouza, A. V. (1990). *The Police Mystique: An Insider's Look at Cops, Crime, and the Criminal Justice System*. New York: Plenum.

Brown, L. P. (1991, February). The Police leadership. *The police chief,* p. 6.

Brown, M. K. (1981). *Working the Street: Discretion and the Dilemmas of Reform*. New York: Russell Sage.

Burns, T., & Stalker, G. M. (1966). *The Management of Innovation*. London: Tavistock.

Carte, G. E., & Carte, E. (1977). O. W. Wilson: Police theory in action. In P. J. Stead (Ed.), *Pioneers in Policing*. Montclair, NJ: Patterson Smith.

Ciampa, D. (1991). *Total Quality: A User's Guide for Implementation*. Reading, MA: Addison-Wesley.

Cohen, H. S., & Feldberg, M. (1991). *Power and Restraint: The Moral Dimension of Police Work*. New York: Praeger.

Cohn, A. W. (Ed.). (1978). *Criminal Justice System Annual: Vol 9. The Future of Policing*. Beverly Hills, CA: Sage.

Cory, B. (1983, May). Police unions jockey for position. *Police Magazine, 6,* 12-14, 17-18.

Couper, D. C., & Lobitz, S. H. (1991a, May). The customer is always right: Applying vision, leadership and the problem-solving method to community-oriented policing. *The Police Chief,* 17-23.

Couper, D. C., & Lobitz, S. H. (1991b). *Quality Policing: The Madison Experience.* Washington, DC: Police Executive Research Forum.

Davis, K. (1950). *Human Society.* New York: Macmillan.

DeCottis, T. A., & Kochan, T. A. (1978). Professionalization and unions in law enforcement. In P. F. Cromwall, Jr. & G. Keefer (Eds.), *Police-Community Relations: Selected Readings* (2nd ed.). St. Paul, MN: West.

Drucker, P. F. (1974). *Management: Tasks, Responsibilities, Practices.* New York: Harper & Row.

Dulaney, W. M. (1984). *Black Shields: A Historical and Comparative Survey of Blacks in American Police Forces.* Unpublished doctoral dissertation, The Ohio State University, Columbus.

Emerson, R. M. (1962). Power-dependence relations. *American Sociological Review, 27,* 31-41.

Enter, J. E. (1986a). Rise to the top: An analysis of police chief career patterns. *Police Science and Administration, 14,* 334-346.

Enter, J. E. (1986b). Role of higher education in the career of the American police chief. *Police Studies, 9,* 110-119.

Eskridge, C. (1989). College and the police: A review of the issues. In D. J. Kenney (Ed.), *Police and Policing* (pp. 17-25). New York: Praeger.

Fallon, D. (1984). Police labor in the '80s. *National Centurion, 2,* 38-45.

Feuille, P., Hendricks, W., & Delaney, J. T. (1983). *The Impact of Collective Bargaining and Interest Arbitration on Policing* (Final Report). Washington, DC: National Institute of Justice.

Fukuda, R. (1983). *Managerial Engineering: Techniques for Improving Quality and Productivity in the Workplace.* Stamford, CT: Productivity, Inc.

Galbraith, J. K. (1967). *The New Industrial State.* Boston: Houghton Mifflin.

Gamson, W. A. (1968). *Power and Discontent.* Homewood, IL: Dorsey.

Gates, D. F. (1992). *Chief: My Life in the LAPD.* New York: Bantam.

Geller, W. A. (Ed.). (1985). *Police Leadership in America: Crisis and Opportunity.* New York: Praeger.

Gerth, H. H., & Mills, C. W. (Eds. & Trans.). (1946). *From Max Weber: Essays in Sociology.* New York: Oxford University Press.

Goldstein, H. (1977). *Policing a Free Society.* Cambridge, MA: Ballinger.

Goldstein, H. (1990). *Problem-Oriented Policing.* New York: McGraw-Hill.

Graham, H. (1988). Ohio's experience with interest arbitration for public sector employees. *Journal of Collective Negotiations in the Public Sector, 17,* 102-113.

Granovetter, M., & Tilly, C. (1988). Inequality and labor processes. In N. J. Smelser (Ed.), *Handbook of Sociology* (pp. 175-221). Beverly Hills, CA: Sage.

Gusfield, J. R. (1963). *Symbolic Crusade: Status Politics and the American Temperance Movement.* Urbana: University of Illinois Press.

Halpern, S. C. (1974, Summer). Police employee organizations and accountability procedures in three cities: Some reflections on police policy-making. *Law and Society Review,* 561-582.

Harvie, R. A., & Lawson, P. E. (1978). Occupational implications of police collective bargaining. *Police Studies, 1,* 24-31.

Henderson, A. R., & Parsons, T. (Eds. & Trans.). (1947). *Max Weber: The Theory of Social and Economic Organization.* New York: Free Press.

Hirschman, A. O. (1970). *Exit, Voice, and Loyalty: Responses to Decline in Firms, Organizations, and States.* Cambridge, MA: Harvard University Press.

Hughes, E. C. (1959). The study of occupations. In R. K. Merton, L. Broom, & L. S. Cottrell (Eds.), *Society Today* (pp. 442-460). New York: Basic Books.

Hunt, R. G. (1987). Coping with racism: Lessons from institutional change in police departments. In J. W. Shaw, P. G. Nordlie, & R. M. Shapiro (Eds.), *Strategies for Improving Race Relations: The Anglo-American Experience* (pp. 5-27). Manchester, UK: Manchester University Press.

Hunt, R. G. (1988). On the metaphysics of choice, or when decisions aren't. In R. Cardy, S. Puffer, & J. Newman (Eds.), *Advances in Information Processing in Organizations* (Vol. 3, pp. 1-23). New York: JAI.

Hunt, R. G., & Magenau, J. M. (1983a). A task analysis strategy for analyzing decision-making in organizations. In L. G. Nigro (Ed.), *Decision Making in Public Organizations* (pp. 117-150). New York: Marcel Dekker.

Hunt, R. G., & Magenau, J. M. (1983b). Value dilemmas in law enforcement: A study of decision-making in a police department. *Law and Policy Quarterly, 5,* 455-477.

Hunt, R. G., McCadden, K. S., & Mordaunt, T. J. (1983). Police roles: Content and conflict. *Journal of Police Science and Administration, 11,* 175-184.

Ichniowski, C., Freeman, R. B., & Lauer, H. (1989). Collective bargaining laws, threat effects, and the determination of police compensation. *Journal of Labor Economics, 7,* 191-209.

Imwald, R., & Kenney, D. J. (1989). Psychological testing of police candidates. In D. J. Kenney (Ed.), *Police and Policing* (pp. 34-44). New York: Praeger.

Jacobs, J. B. (1985). Police unions: How they look from the academic side. In W. A. Geller (Ed.), *Police Leadership in America: Crisis and Opportunity* (pp. 286-292). New York: Praeger.

Janowitz, M. (1961). Hierarchy and authority in the military establishment. In A. Etzioni (Ed.), *Complex Organizations: A Sociological Reader* (pp. 198-211). New York: Holt, Rinehart and Winston.

Jermier, J., Cohen, C. F., Powers, K. J., & Gaines, J. (1988). Paying dues: Police unionism in a "right-to-work" environment. *Industrial Relations, 25,* 265-275.

Joiner, R. (1985). The key role of statisticians in the transformation of North American industry. *The American Statistician, 39,* 223-234.

Juris, H. A., & Feuille, P. (1973). *The Impact of Police Unions: Summary Report.* Washington, DC: LEAA/NILECJ.

Katz, D., & Kahn, R. L. (1978). *The Social Psychology of Organizing* (2nd ed.). New York: Wiley.

Keenoy, T. (1981). The employment relationship as a form of socio-economic exchange. In G. Dlugos & K. Weiermair (Eds.), *Management Under Different Value Systems* (pp. 406-446). New York: De Gruyter.

Kelling, G., Pate, T., Dieckman, D., & Brown, C. E. (1974). *The Kansas City Preventive Patrol Experiment: Technical Report.* Washington, DC: Police Foundation.

Kerstetter, W. A. (1985). Who disciplines the police? Who should? In W. A. Geller (Ed.), *Police Leadership in America* (pp. 149-182, 196-200). New York: Praeger.

Kieser, A. (1989). Organizational, institutional, and societal evolution: Medieval crafts guilds and the genesis of formal organizations. *Administrative Science Quarterly, 34,* 540-564.

Kilmann, R. H., Saxton, M. J., Serpa, R., & associates. (1985). *Gaining Control of the Corporate Culture.* San Francisco: Jossey-Bass.

Kipnis, D. (1976). *The Powerholders.* Chicago: University of Chicago Press.

Kleinman, D. M. (1979). Zinging it to the chief. *Police Magazine, 2,* 39-44.

Kleismet, R. B. (1985). The chief and the union: May the force be with you. In W. A. Geller (Ed.), *Police Leadership in America* (pp. 281-285). New York: Praeger.

Klockars, C. B. (1985). Order maintenance, the quality of urban life, and police: A different line of argument. In W. A. Geller (Ed.), *Police Leadership in America* (pp. 309-321). New York: Praeger.

Klockars, C. B. (1992, May 15). The only way to make real progress in controlling excessive force by police. *Law Enforcement News, 18*, pp. 12, 18.

Levi, M. A. (1977). *Bureaucratic Insurgency: The Case of Police Unions.* Lexington, MA: Heath.

Levine, M. J. (1988). Historical overview of police unionization in the United States. *Police Journal, 61,* 334-343.

Magenau, J. M., & Hunt, R. G. (1989). Sociopolitical networks for police role-making. *Human Relations, 42,* 547-560.

Magenau, J. M., & Hunt, R. G. (1992). *Police Unions, the Police Role, and Police Role Outcomes.* Penn-State, Erie, School of Business, Working Paper Series # 92-5.

Manning, P. K. (1977). *Police Work: The Social Organization of Policing.* Cambridge: MIT Press.

Manning, P. K. (1983). Policing and technology: Technologies and the police. In M. Tonry & N. Morris (Eds.), *Modern Policing,* Volume 5 of Crime and Justice Annuals. Chicago: University of Chicago Press.

Manning, P. K., & Hawkins, K. (1989). Police decision-making. In M. W. Weatheritt (Ed.), *Police Research: Some Future Prospects* (pp. 139-156). Aldershot, UK: Avebury.

Martin, S. (1989). Women in policing: The eighties and beyond. In D. J. Kenney (Ed.), *Police and Policing: Contemporary Issues.* New York: Praeger.

Mayo, L. A. (1985). Leading blindly: An assessment of chief's information about police operations. In W. A. Geller (Ed.), *Police Leadership in America* (pp. 397-417). New York: Praeger.

McLaughlin, V., & Bing, R. (1989). Selection, training, and discipline of police officers. In D. J. Kenney (Ed.), *Police and Policing* (pp. 26-33). New York: Praeger.

McNamara, J. D. (1990). *The Blue Mirage.* New York: Morrow.

McNeill, W. H. (1982). *The Pursuit of Power: Technology, Armed Force, and Society Since A.D. 1000.* Chicago: University of Chicago Press.

Meindl, J. R., & Ehrlich, S. (1987). The romance of leadership and the evaluation of organization performance. *Academy of Management Journal, 30,* 91-109.

Metcalf, H. C., & Urwick, L. (Eds.). (1941). *Dynamic Administration, the Collected Papers of Mary Parker Follett.* New York: Harper & Row.

Meyer, J. M., & Rowan, B. (1977). Institutionalized organizations: Formal structure as myth and ceremony. *American Journal of Sociology, 83,* 340-363.

Miller, D., & Friesen, P. H. (1984). *Organizations: A Quantum View.* Englewood Cliffs, NJ: Prentice-Hall.

Mintzberg, H. (1979). *The Structuring of Organizations.* Englewood Cliffs, NJ: Prentice-Hall.

Mintzberg, H. (1983). *Power In and Around Organizations.* Englewood Cliffs, NJ: Prentice-Hall.

Monkkonen, E. H. (1981). *Police in Urban America 1860-1920.* New York: Cambridge University Press.

Moore, M. H., & Kelling, G. L. (1983, Winter). To serve and protect: Learning from police history. *The Public Interest, 70,* 49-65.

More, H. W. (1992). *Challenging Police Management: The Evolution and Impact of Police Unions.* Cincinnati, OH: Anderson.

Muir, W. K., Jr. (1977). *Police: Streetcorner Politicians.* Chicago: University of Chicago Press.

Murphy, P. V. (1977). *Commissioner: A View from the Top of American Law Enforcement.* New York: Simon & Schuster.

Napper, G. (1985). Who disciplines the police? I do! A response to Wayne Kerstetter. In W. A. Geller (Ed.), *Police Leadership in America* (pp. 193-195). New York: Praeger.

Neilsen, S. C. (1990, April). The trouble with "political trouble." *The Police Chief,* 141-144.

Ouchi, W. (1979). *Theory Z: How American Business Can Meet the Japanese Challenge.* Reading, MA: Addison-Wesley.

Parsons, T. (1960). *Structure and Process in Modern Societies.* New York: Free Press.

Perrow, C. (1979). *Complex Organizations: A Critical Essay* (2nd ed.). Glenview, IL: Scott-Foresman.

Pfeffer, J. (1992). *Managing With Power: Politics and Influence in Organizations.* Boston: Harvard Business School Press.

Pfeffer, J., & Salancik, G. R. (1978). *The External Control of Organizations: A Resource Dependence Approach.* New York: Harper & Row.

Pisani, A. (1992, May 15). Dissecting community policing—Part 1. *Law Enforcement News,* p. 13.

Pomeroy, W. A. C. (1985). The sources of police legitimacy and a model for police misconduct review: A response to Wayne Kerstetter. In W. A. Geller (Ed.), *Police Leadership in America* (pp. 183-186). New York: Praeger.

President's Commission on Law Enforcement and Administration of Justice. (1967). *Task Force Report: The Police.* Washington, DC: U.S. Government Printing Office.

Price, R. B. (1977). *Criminal Justice Research: New Models and Findings.* Beverly Hills, CA: Sage.

Pugh, M. P. (1980). *The Effect of Unionization vs Non-unionization on Wage Determination in Municipal Police Agencies With One Hundred or More Sworn and Non-sworn Personnel.* Washington, DC: National Institute of Justice/National Criminal Justice Reference Service.

Reiner, R. (1978). *The Blue-Coated Worker: A Sociological Study of Police Unionism.* London: Cambridge University Press.

Reuss-Ianni, E. (1983). *Two Cultures of Policing: Street Cops and Management Cops.* New Brunswick, NJ: Transaction Books.

Roethlisberger, F., & Dickson, W. (1939). *Management and the Worker.* Cambridge, MA: Harvard University Press.

Rumbaut, R. G., & Bittner, E. (1979). Changing conceptions of the police role. In N. Morris & M. Tonry (Eds.), *Crime and Justice: Vol. 1. An Annual Review of Research.* Chicago: University of Chicago Press.

Rynecki, S. A., Cairns, D. A., & Cairns, D. J. (1978). *Police Collective Bargaining Agreements: A National Management Survey.* Washington, DC: Police Executive Research Forum.

Rynecki, S. A., & Morse, M. J. (1981). *Police Collective Bargaining Agreements: A National Management Survey* (rev. ed.). Washington, DC: Police Executive Research Forum.

Salerno, C. A. (1981). *Police at the Bargaining Table.* Springfield, IL: Thomas.

Scaff, L. A. (1989). *Fleeing the Iron Cage: Culture, Politics, and Modernity in the Thought of Max Weber.* Berkeley: University of California Press.

Schwartz, A. (1985). Reaching systemic police abuses—The need for civilian investigation of misconduct: A response to Wayne Kerstetter. In W. A. Geller (Ed.), *Police Leadership in America* (pp. 187-192). New York: Praeger.

Scott, W. R. (1987). The adolescence of institutional theory. *Administrative Science Quarterly, 32,* 493-511.

Selznick, P. (1957). *Leadership in Administration.* New York: Harper & Row.

Sherman, L. W. (1978). *The Quality of Police Education.* San Francisco: Jossey-Bass.

Smelser, N. J. (Ed.). (1988). *Handbook of Sociology* (pp. 175-221). Beverly Hills, CA: Sage.

Stead, P. J. (1977). *Pioneers in Policing.* Montclair, NJ: Patterson Smith.

Stone, L. (1991, August 12). Review of Paul Johnson, *The Birth of the Modern: World Society 1815-30. The New Republic,* 36-40.

Swimmer, G. (1983). The impact of Proposition 13 on municipal police in California. *Journal of Collective Negotiations in the Public Sector, 12,* 127-134.

Taylor, F. W. (1947). *Scientific Management.* New York: Harper & Row. (Originally published in 1911)

Thompson, J. D. (1967). *Organizations in Action.* New York: McGraw-Hill.

Thompson, O. M. (1988). *A Study of Emerging Militancy of Police Unions.* Unpublished doctoral dissertation, University of Southern California, Los Angeles.

Van de Ven, A., & Astley, W. G. (1981). Mapping the field to create a dynamic perspective on organizational design and behavior. In A. H. Van de Ven & W. F. Joyce (Eds.), *Perspectives on Organization Design and Behavior* (pp. 427-468). New York: Wiley.

Vollmer, A. (1971). *The Police and Modern Society.* Montclair, NJ: Patterson Smith. (Originally published in 1936)

Walder, A. G. (1986). *Communist Neo-Traditionalism: Work and Authority in Chinese Industry.* Berkeley: University of California Press.

Walker, S. (1983). *The Police in America.* New York: McGraw-Hill.

Walker, S. (1985). Setting the standards: The efforts and impact of blue-ribbon commissions on the police. In W. A. Geller (Ed.), *Police Leadership in America* (pp. 351-353). New York: Praeger.

Walton, M. (1986). *The Deming Management Method.* New York: Putnam.

Weick, K. (1979). *The Social Psychology of Organizing* (2nd ed.). Reading, MA: Addison-Wesley.

William O. Douglas Institute for the Study of Contemporary Social Problems. (1984, January). *The Future of Policing: A Panel Report.* Seattle, WA: Douglas Institute.

Wilson, J. Q. (1968). *Varieties of Police Behavior: The Management of Law and Order in Eight Communities.* Cambridge, MA: Harvard University Press.

Wilson, J. Q. (1989). *Bureaucracy: What Government Agencies Do and Why They Do It.* New York: Basic Books.

Wilson, J. Q., & Kelling, G. L. (1982, March). Police and neighborhood safety: Broken windows. *Atlantic Monthly, 249,* 29-38.

Wilson, O. W. (1963). *Police Administration* (2nd ed.). New York: McGraw-Hill.

Witham, D. C., & Watson, P. J. (Undated). *The Role of the Law Enforcement Executive.* Management Science Unit, FBI Academy, Federal Bureau of Investigation, U.S. Department of Justice.

Wycoff, M. A. (1982). *The Role of Municipal Police Research as a Prelude to Changing It* (Technical Report to National Institute of Justice). Washington, DC: Police Foundation.

Zucker, L. (1987). Institutional theories of organization. *Annual Review of Sociology, 13,* 443-464.

Index

About the Authors

Raymond G. Hunt is Professor of Organization and Human Resources in the School of Management and Director of The Center for Industrial Effectiveness, State University of New York at Buffalo. He received his Ph.D. (in Psychology) from the University of Buffalo. He was previously Professor at Cornell University and Washington University (St. Louis), and a Fellow of the William O. Douglas Institute for the Study of Contemporary Social Problems (Seattle). He is a specialist in organizational assessment, general management, decision-making, the structuring of organizations, and organizational and public policy. He is also the author of numerous scientific, technical, and professional books and articles. He has extensive applied research and consulting experience with both large and small organizations in the private, public, and voluntary sectors of the United States and abroad.

John M. Magenau received his Ph.D. in 1981 from the State University of New York at Buffalo. He has published several research articles and book chapters on negotiation and dispute resolution, worker's patterns of commitment to employer and union, and decision-making processes in police departments. An associate professor and director to the School of Business at Penn State Erie, The Behrend College, he is also a research associate of the William O. Douglas Institute for the Study of Contemporary Social Problems.